yes!

Yes! Inc.
1035 31st St. NW
Washington, DC
20007-4482
(202) 338-7874
(202) 338-2727

Illuminations

A Guide to Essential Buddhist Practices

SAKYA PANDITA

Translated by
Geshe Wangyal and Brian Cutillo

LOTSAWA

Library of Congress Cataloging in Publication Data

Sa-skya Pandi-ta Kun-dga' rgyal-mtshan, 1182-1251.
    Illuminations: a guide to essential Buddhist practices.

    Translation of: Thub pa'i dgons pa rab tu gsal ba.
    Bibliography: p. 141
    Includes index.
    1. Religious life—Sa-skya-pa (Sect)—Early works to 1800. 2. Sa-skya-pa (Sect)—Doctrines—Early works to 1800.   I. Thupten Wangyal.   II. Cutillo, Brian.   III. Title.
BQ7672.6.S23   1987   294.3'4448   87-36622
ISBN 0-932156-05-3

Production: Matrix Productions
Text Design: Merrill Peterson
Cover Design: Mattie Avalon
Copy Editing: Vicki Nelson
Word Processing: Wordsworth & Kim Freeman
Typesetting: Harrington-Young

Printed in the United States of America

9 8 7 6 5 4 3 2 1

In Memoriam
KENNETH G. COLSTAD

I asked so much of you
In this brief lifetime,
Perhaps we'll meet again
In the childhood of the next.

—The Love Poems of the Sixth Dalai Lama

Contents

Preface

Illuminations is a useful, down-to-earth guide for beginning the process of mental and spiritual development as taught and enacted by the historical Buddha Śākyamuni and succeeding masters of India, Tibet, and the world. Neither abstruse nor mystical, it is directed toward those who wish to lay the necessary groundwork for advanced practice.

But why did the author, the famous Tibetan personality Sakya Pandita, feel a need to "clarify Buddha's intentions," as his Tibetan title states? The words of the Śākyamuni are believed to be fairly well preserved in the enormous collection called *The Three Baskets*. These three divisions comprise the canonical scripture: sutra (practice), discipline (code of conduct), and illuminating science (theories of mind and the physical world). Although these scriptures are taken as "gospel," they were written down after being preserved for several hundred years of oral transmission and are somewhat unsystematic in structure. They are also records of what Śākyamuni taught to specific persons and audiences, and because they reflect the cultural context of his time, they do not in themselves provide a clear, integrated, and unambiguous explanation of the particulars of spiritual practice. Therefore, later masters in India refined the material of the scriptures in texts called śāstras.

Later, after the buddhist religion was well established in Tibet, native teachers wrote their own commentaries on these scriptures and texts.

Sakya Pandita cast the present work in the form of a "stages of the path" (*lam rim*) teaching. Such teachings are a reformulation of Śākyamuni's words into a complete and integrated system of practice. Sakya Pandita's presentation is comprehensive, yet it retains the informal flavor of a transcription of lectures for an introduction to basic buddhism.

Why did we feel it important to translate and publish this particular work? Buddhism has influenced Western thought for centuries. In America it has had a strong impact upon the thought of Emerson, Thoreau, Jefferson, and many others. In the 1960s and 1970s interest increased, and currently hundreds of buddhist text translations from various languages and traditions are in print. Many are of excellent scholarship, and a few are truly beautifully rendered. Most, however, are either scholarly works, canonical scripture difficult to interpret in terms of everyday practice, or treatises far too advanced for meaningful application by most people. *Illuminations* attempts to fill this gap by providing a practical manual of essential buddhist practices in a clear and direct style. This was also Sakya Pandita's purpose in the thirteenth century, and the book has been translated with his aim in mind. Some alterations have been made in the format of the text, but not in its content.

The work of translation began in 1970 with a reading of the text by the late Geshe Wangyal to several close students at his retreat house in Washington, New Jersey. In 1977, Bea Ferrigno assisted in revising and editing the text. In the fall of 1985 I once again turned to the translation, but felt that the manner of presentation was too formal for its intended audience in America. Recalling Geshe Wangyal's exhortation to "do it *properly*," I decided to move certain portions of the text into a separate section, Part Two, leaving the essential "stages of the path" material in Part One. Thus Part One can be thought of as a handbook for practice and Part Two as autocommentary and notes. The bold, bracketed numbers in Part One mark places in the original text from which material has been extracted. These extracts comprise Part Two. A few passages were omitted entirely, or made into footnotes. But most important, language and style were made as clear and concise as possible without compromising the text.

Sakya Pandita's own notes in Part One are asterisked at the bottom of the page; our explanatory notes there are numbered. Works quoted by Sakya Pandita may be identified in text by the following abbreviations:

CS = *The Crown of Great Vehicle Sutras*
EBP = *Entering the Bodhisattva's Practice*
EVC = *Exposition of Valid Cognition*
EW = *Essential Wisdom*
FS = *The Five Stages*
KC = *The King of Concentrations Sutra*
LPE = *The Lamp of the Path to Enlightenment*
PG = *The Precious Garland*
PP = *The Peerless Principle*
RVMW = *Root Verses on the Middle Way*
SB = *The State of Buddhahood*
TA = *The Treasury of Abhidharma*
TWS = *The One Hundred Thousand Verse*
          Transcendent Wisdom Sutra
VT = *The Vajra Tip Sutra*
WT = *The Wheel of Time Tantra*

I have also added excerpts from *Entering the Bodhisattva's Practice* where relevant as a supplement to Sakya Pandita's text. These additions are bracketed and followed by the notation (EBP). We have not been able to identify some of the texts mentioned by the author and have therefore not included them in the list of works cited.

We would like to thank Bea Ferrigno, Myles and Roseann Fowler-White, and Kimberley and Merrill Peterson for editorial development, Douglas Rhoton and William Kirtz for unpublished biographical material on the author, and Daniel C. Kennedy and William C. Mullich for encouragement and support.

Introduction

The Text

On arriving in Tibet in the year 1042, the renowned Indian teacher Atīśa found the buddhist scene in a confused, developmental state. The Indian religious system was foreign to Tibetans, and its adherents were involved in a multitude of divergent, unsystematic practices. Atīśa was a master of the two great vehicle (*mahāyāna*) traditions derived from Śākyamuni's teachings: the tradition of "profound view" originated by Nāgārjuna (second/third century) and the tradition of "extensive deeds" stemming from the teachings of Asaṅga and Vasubandhu (fourth/fifth century). He was also skilled in the teachings of the lesser vehicle (*hīnayāna*) and the tantric vehicle (*vajrayāna*), though these played a secondary role in his work in Tibet. Atīśa's consummate gift to the Tibetan people was his teaching of an integrated, continuous path, organizing into systematic stages of practice the seemingly divergent lesser vehicle, the two great vehicle traditions, and the esoteric tantric vehicles.

Such a teaching came to be known as "stages of the path," or more loosely, "stages of practice." This teaching was presented in Atīśa's seminal work *The Lamp of the Path to Enlightenment* (Bodhipathapradīpam), composed especially for the Tibetan people. This integrated approach became one of the primary models for buddhist practice in Tibet. Its subsequent development there constitutes one of the greatest Tibetan contributions to the evolution of Dharma, exemplifying their comprehensive and impartial overview of the various traditions of Indian buddhism. At the turn of the twelfth century the learned Tibetan Gampopa (sGam-po-pa, 1079-1153), Milarepa's successor in the Kagyupa lineage, composed a well-known "stages of the path" titled *The Jewel Ornament of Liberation*, an extremely concise and well-written text. Later, the reformer Tsongkapa (1357-1419) wrote his magnum opus, *The Great Stages of the Path*, using Atīśa's work as a root text. He extended the integrated path approach into the tantric tradition in *The Great Stages of the Mantric Path*.

Between the writing of these two works, the unique teacher and scholar Kun-dga' rGyal-mtsham, more popularly known as Sakya Pandita, wrote *Illuminating Buddha's Thought* (*thub pa'i dgongs pa rab tu gsal ba*), translated here as *Illuminations*. This "stages of the path" is neither as concise as Gampopa's work nor as definitive as Tsongkapa's; it is meant in its own way to serve the needs of Sakya Pandita's students and, as he adds, "of all the world." This work remains one of the primary teaching books of the Sakya order and others, who refer to it as "the Sakyas' Stages of the Path."

The Author

Sakya Pandita was the spiritual descendent of the colorful and eccentric Tibetan yogin Drokmi ('Brog-mi, 992-1074), who brought from India the lineage that evolved into the Sakya order. Drokmi was, for a time, the teacher of Translator Marpa, the founder of the Kagyupa order. In India, Drokmi studied with the famous teacher Śāntipa, from whom he received *The Hevajra Tantra*, which later became the central tantra of the Sakya; and with Dombi Heruka, from whom he received the teachings called "path and result" (*lam 'bras*), which became the model for Sakya practice.

Drokmi's successor was Konchog Gyelpo (dKon-mchok rgyal-po), who established the main monastery of the order of Sakya near Shigatse in 1073. *Sakya* means "grey earth," so called because of the color of the soil, which was considered auspicious. (It was, however, also on a main well-traveled trade route.) Later, after it had become a thriving religious and political center, the Sakya monastery was presided over by Sakya Pandita and his successor 'Phags-pa. Because of their influence with the Mongols, the Sakyas maintained this zenith of political power for a period of over one-hundred years, from 1245 to 1358. This ascendancy was weakened by the death of Kublai Khan in 1294, and was ended by the collapse of the Mongol reign in China (1358-1360).

In the religious realm Sakya Pandita taught oral teachings extending from Drokmi. He systematized the practice of *Hevajra* and *Samvara* tantras and formulated the "path and result" teachings into an integrated practice for attaining enlightenment in one lifetime, based on the tetrad of correct view of voidness, meditation practice, ritual, and fulfillment.

Although much reduced in size and influence, the Sakya order remains to this day one of the four main orders of Tibetan buddhism and, though now the smallest, it preserves the integrity and vitality of its teachings and practices. The Sakya order maintains tantric as well as great vehicle traditions in the "path and result" practices, and its teachings are known for their excellence and breadth of scholarship as well as, on a personal level, their fundamentally humanistic approach.

Sakya Pandita's birth in the year 1182 was, according to tradition, accompanied by auspicious omens. Bright lights and rainbows filled the sky over Sakya Valley, and a multitude of dakinis watched as a rain of flowers fell to earth. His linguistic abilities were evident at a very early age. As a child he could speak Sanskrit and write its alphabet with sticks on the ground. In youth he excelled in the arts and medicine, receiving instructions from the Bodhisattva Mañjuśrī in dreams; he later became a renowned artist. By the age of eighteen Sakya Pandita was already active in the propagation of buddhism, clearing up the misconceptions of teachers and scholars of the time. His knowledge of the mental science of Abhidharma is said to have been communicated to him in a dream by the Indian master Vasubandhu.

By the age of twenty-seven Sakya Pandita had mastered the teachings of the great vehicle and tantric vehicle and had received ordination as a full monk. He then undertook the composition of many works dealing with philosophy, art, mental science, and logic. His famous work on epistemology (*pramana*), *The Treasury of Logic*, was the only technical work of Tibetan origin to be translated into Sanskrit and widely circulated in India. His collection of homespun maxims, *The Treasury of Precious Sayings*, is still popular among the common people of Tibet. Sakya Pandita made a science of the Indian custom of debate. He was usually successful at such formal debates, and the posture in which he is usually depicted shows one of the stylized gestures used.

In 1244, Godan Khan, the grandson of Gengis Khan and ruler of the militaristic Mongol nation, heard about the new Tibetan religion and requested that a teacher be sent to his court. Sakya Pandita was chosen for the job and succeeded in converting Godan Khan to buddhism. He assisted in the development of a Mongolian script and initiated the translation of buddhist texts into Mongolian. His skill as a politician was evident in his negotiations with the Mongols, as he prevented their invasion of Tibet while enlisting their aid in unifying the country's feudal splinter-kingdoms under a central government. Sakya Pandita himself never ruled the unified country, but before his death he conferred spiritual and political successorship upon his chief disciple, his nephew Chos-rgyal 'Phags-pa, who then led the country in the manner of an Indian spiritual ruler (*dharmarāja*), appointing a lay regent to administer the government matters while 'Phags-pa remained in China to maintain peaceful relations with the Mongols by serving as Kublai Khan's spiritual advisor.

Sakya Pandita spent his own closing years in China as advisor to the ruler, and it was in this self-imposed exile that he composed the text of *Illuminations*. In his old age he spent most of his time instructing his close disciples until his death in 1251. Some of his close disciples reported him to be attended at his death by various bodhisattvas and Indian masters. The yogin Virupa, considered to be an Indian patriarch by the Sakya sect, put in an appearance and predicted Sakya Pandita's rebirth on a distant planet.

Summary of the Text

In his opening words, Sakya Pandita underscores the unifying motif of his work—the intent for enlightenment—in his own verse, followed by a concise outline of the chapter topics taken from *The Crown of Great Vehicle Sutras* by Maitreya/Asanga.

Sakya Pandita's description of the process of spiritual development begins at the beginning: "If you *really* want to begin buddhist practice, you must first understand the motivation for spiritual development." He goes on to present the sequence of practices from a humanistic perspective unique to the Sakya sect. The progression of topics follows the "stages of the path" format, covering the same ground as Gampopa's *The Jewel Ornament of Liberation*, but in a more informal and informative style. Sakya Pandita draws on two important Indian works to structure his discourse: Maitreya/Asanga's *Crown of Great Vehicle Sutras* and Sāntideva's *Entering the Bodhisattva's Practice*. He places particular emphasis on the "intent for enlightenment" (*bodhicitta*), which is the unifying theme of Sāntideva's exquisite poem; and thus, he quotes freely from that work. Sakya Pandita tends to dwell more on essential practices for beginning and intermediate practitioners than Sāntideva does, providing many valuable tips or "keys" for making practice fruitful.

The author has decorated his text with numerous quotations from all sorts of texts and sutras. They should not be allowed to distract from the thematic line of the text itself. Frequently such quotations are used to shore up an author's argument, but this does not seem to be the case here. In this work they serve to acquaint the reader with a surprising number of the most important buddhist treatises and should serve, along with the Eastern/Western bibliography provided at the end of the book, as a valuable resource. Although we have attempted to make the work self-sufficient, a brief synopsis of the topics may be helpful.

Chapter 1 deals with the impulse for spiritual, or mental, development (the two terms are synonymous here), the types of practitioners and their reasons for attempting to practice, and the role of the inherent discomfort of the human condition.

Chapter 2   explains the first formal step in Buddhist practice: taking refuge in the triple gem (Buddha as exemplar of the liberated person, the Dharma which is his teaching, and the Sangha or community of practitioners who provide support in this difficult endeavor).

Chapter 3   explains the intent for enlightenment as the in-grained impulse to obtain one's own liberation in order to help others to do likewise. It is the major prerequisite for advanced practice in both the great vehicle and the tantric vehicle. However, the author reserves his personal instructions for the actual generation of the intent for enlightenment for a later chapter on meditative absorption. To round out the chapter, we have included at the end an extended quote from the remarkable third chapter of Śāntideva's *Entering the Bodhisattva's Practice*.

Chapter 4   deals with the six transcendences (*pāramitā*) that form the core of the book and of buddhist practice itself. These six categories of practice include all essential great vehicle techniques and form an interlocking system for focusing one's energies toward the goal of liberation. They are the means for acquiring the two accumulations: that of personal power or merit through refine-ment of behavior, and that of wisdom or gnosis through refinement of knowledge in meditation. These two accumulations or stores are complementary and mutually supportive. The practices associated with the six transcendences are not "transcendent" until they are practiced with transcendent wisdom—the experiential realization of the natural state, or voidness, of everything. But even before this goal is reached they are useful. At the outset of practice, the first three—giving, moral behavior, and patience—provide the basis for development by correcting our overvaluation of ourselves and providing the conducive conditions created by correct lifestyle, as well as by granting endurance in the face of the hardships and intense experiences of advanced practice. The fourth, effort, serves as a stimulus to all the others by creating the inspiration and energy for the process of development.

The material in the chapters on transcendent meditative absorption and wisdom is extensive. Section 4.5 is a continuation of the discussion of the intent for enlightenment begun in Chapter 3, rather than an exposition of the system for attaining the states of meditative absorption through concentration, which would be the topic expected here. (The subject of meditative absorption is covered in Chapter 6.4.1, the section on the mundane meditation path.) Now the text really catches fire. Interweaving his own discourse with verses from Śāntideva's *Entering the Bodhisattva's Practice*, Sakya Pandita gives valuable instructions and tips for practice from a very personal standpoint. He presents the two major techniques for generating the intent for enlightenment. The first technique is the meditation on all beings as one's mother. This is, in fact, a recognition of the interconnectedness of all life that propels the development of love and compassion, and, finally, the actual intent. The second technique is the method of exchange of self and others, with its preparatory meditation on the equivalence of self and others. This is a quicker, more effective method that is not well known in the West because of a reluctance on the part of present-day teachers who are concerned with its potential dangers to the practitioner. His masterful treatment of this topic is certainly one of the most valuable sections of the book.

If Section 4.5 is the heart of the book, Section 4.6 is the nerve center. Here the author provides information about the central experience of buddhism: the realization of the natural state of everything—voidness—the fact that every phenomenon does not actually exist in the way it is perceived by the ordinary conditioned mind. This nerve center activates and illuminates the practices of the other five transcendences. It is also the most misunderstood aspect of buddhist doctrine in Tibet and the West. The experience of voidness serves as a necessary counterweight to balance the emphasis on compassion. Compassion, and the first five transcendences, in the absence of "wisdom" will only serve to bind one to the ordinary world of samsara, although it is conversely true that wisdom and the experience of voidness alone will bind one to the lesser nirvana and the practitioner will also ultimately fail to achieve enlightenment. Thus, Sakya Pandita emphasizes the importance of correct intellectual understanding of "view" and correct utilization of the experience in the course of practice, as is taught in teachings of the "stages of the path." He begins the chapter with a discussion of several practices and theories popular in his time, and, not surprisingly, remarkably similar to some current trends in the West. Many of these resemble the "Mere Blankness Is Sufficient" school of the Chinese monk Hashang, and the arguments presented here should be of interest to modern readers. The second part of the chapter deals with the main theories concerning the nature of the world and its reality (the two truths), and the important features of the meditative practice and how it fits into the course of development. The frequency with which the discussion turns to the practice of *mahāmudrā* probably reflects the author's basically tantric stance, although that lies beyond the formal scope of the text.

The analysis of self and environment that is the core of transcendent wisdom practice leads to the direct experiential realization of the true pattern of existence, the natural state, the flash-perception of voidness (the experience of *śūnyatā*). From this point the practice is known as the path of insight and the meditation path, and these are the topics of Chapter 6.

Chapter 5   concerns the four social means, a seldom-discussed subject that forms a kind of extension to the preceding sections on the transcendences. Whereas the six transcendences are practiced primarily for one's own advancement, the four social means are aimed specifically at other beings. They consist of four types of social skills by which the bodhisattva helps others achieve their own goals, especially, but not limited to, spiritual aims.

Chapter 6   leaves the province of basic practice and undertakes advanced development. The topic of the five paths ranges over the entirety of buddhist practice and development from yet another point of view. All of the material covered so far comprises the first two paths—the accumulation and application paths. In the former are included all practices aimed at behavioral development and acquisition of knowledge directed at liberation. In the latter, the practices aimed at experiencing voidness (*śūnyatā*) are also included.

The author explains the "path" as process: each path consists of repeated interlocking phases of practice and resultant experience through which the practitioner must pass many times. After accumulating the stores of personal power through behavioral development and acquisition of knowledge of the accumulation path and after sufficient success in practicing the meditations on voidness of the application path, the so-called superior development (*āryamarga*) commences with the first flash-experience of voidness. This signals the start of the third path—the insight path. The insight path process consists of repeated experiences of voidness, each one preceded by a period of meditative preparation and is followed by what is called the post-realization state. As the manifold conditions that have been imposed on our mind since birth are one by one removed by the impact of these experiences, the hard ground of our ingrained, rigid way of seeing ourselves and the world is gradually loosened during in the post-realization periods.

Sakya Pandita has divided the section on the fourth path, the so-called meditation path, into two separate and unrelated topics. One is the mundane meditation path, which deals with the basic practice of attaining the various levels or modes of mental function termed "absorptions" through the practice of concentration. The other is the transcendent meditation path, which extends the analysis of "acquired conditionings" performed on the insight path to "innate conditionings." During this process the realization states gradually merge into the post-realization state, producing almost constant experience of the natural state. The fifth is the final path, or the "path beyond practice," and consists of one process of final tolerance followed by the final realization, which is synonymous with enlightenment or buddhahood. Both emotional and cognitive obscurations are totally eliminated, along with all tendencies that they occur again.

But realization is only half the story. During the course of development a bodhisattva must also develop the "three bodies" of a buddha.

Chapter 7   deals with the "ten bodhisattva stages," which begin when the insight path is first achieved and extend to final buddhahood. These ten stages of development culminate in the form body of a buddha, whereas the five paths culminate in the reality body of realization. This discussion leads naturally into the next chapter.

Chapter 8   is a fairly comprehensive exposition of the special qualities that distinguish a Buddha's enlightenment. In particular, Sakya Pandita takes care to differentiate those qualities that distinguish a real buddha from an arhat who achieves nirvana through the lesser vehicles. It is not just a difference of degree or range of ability, but in most instances it is a difference in kind. Several examples are important to note. Arhats of the lesser vehicle have indeed conquered their afflictions—the largely emotional negativities that plague humanity. They have not, however, eliminated the traces or imprintings that, though unconscious, will in time develop into afflictive mental states again. The nirvana of the lesser vehicle is considered to be a temporary and not very desirable state, although for those who are unusually upset at the human condition it can be a waystation on the way to enlightenment where one may rest a while. A buddha is bound neither to the miseries of the samsaric condition nor to the extension of nirvana. In enlightenment one achieves true freedom from one or the other by removing the automatic, compulsive workings of the mind. One is free to chose, and a buddha chooses to continue in this world, exercising all his hard-won abilities, knowledge, and realization in the campaign to win freedom for everyone.

PART ONE

Path, Practices, and Goal

Sakya Pandita's Preface

Respectful homage to Guru and Mañjughoṣa

Perfect buddhas, source of help and happiness,
Are born from bodhisattvas.
Bodhisattvas are born from the essential
Compassion and voidness of the intent for enlightenment.
Out of reverence for the intent to achieve
Enlightenment for the sake of helping others
I will briefly explain the stages of practice
Of the bodhisattva's good path.

In striving to attain peerless, real, perfect enlightenment, the intelligent ones, the bodhisattvas, produce the intent for enlightenment. In this book I will explain the stages of the path as outlined thus in *The Crown of Great Vehicle Sutras*:

Inclination for and involvement in Dharma,
Production of the intent for enlightenment,
Practice of giving and the other [transcendences],
Aiding the development of beings,
Entering the faultless, and
Purification of the environment,
Unconditioned nirvana,
Supreme enlightenment and teacher.

1

The Inclination
for Spiritual Development

If you really want to start buddhist practice, you should first understand your inclination for spiritual development, the foundation of practice.[1] *The Crown of Great Vehicle Sutras* explains that there are natural and cultivated types of spiritual inclination:

Natural and cultivated inclinations
Are the support and the supported.
Their presence, absence, and advantages
Should be known for the sake of liberation.

Natural inclination exists in all people and supports cultivated inclination, which exists only through production of the intent for enlightenment. The signs of spiritual inclination are the presence of compassion prior to spiritual practice, interest in the Three Jewels, patience when harmed by others, and a natural tendency to behave virtuously. These are the signs of a person [with the natural inclination] of the buddha family. There are four types of hindrance to spiritual inclination. Habituation to negative emo-

---

[1]The Sanskrit term *gotra*, meaning lineage, family, or race, is rendered here as "spiritual inclination" for clarity.

tions and attitudes produces obsession with food and passions as well as attachment and dislike for beings. Bad friends and relatives, and association with false teachers, can prevent involvement in true Dharma or cause involvement in false Dharma. Poverty can cause discouragement about spiritual practice, and being controlled by others can be an obstruction, as Canakya said [in his *Maxims*]:

> In youth one is controlled by parents,
> In middle-age by one's mate,
> And in old age by one's children—
> Such fools always lack independence.

Spiritual inclination can be temporarily impaired in four ways: lack of circumstances conducive to spirituality, periods of bad behavior [caused by extenuating circumstances], weakening of the seeds of spirituality, or their failure to sprout caused by lack of the moisture of virtuousness. *

---

* The Mind Only school (*Cittamatra*) holds the theory that some people have a permanent lack of spiritual inclination (*agotra*), but the Middle Way school does not. Essentially, anyone who believes that samsara is endless assumes a permanent lack of inclination—SP.

2

Starting Practice

What Is Refuge?

Involvement in spiritual practices means taking refuge, which means to rely on superior objective. In buddhism the refuge objects are the Three Jewels: the Buddha as teacher, the Dharma as the teachings, and the Sangha as the spiritual community of practicers. The basic formula of the refuge vows in Sanskrit, Tibetan, and English pronunciation is:

Buddham sharanam gacchami.
Sangye la gyap su chio.
I take refuge in Buddha.

Dharmam sharanam gacchami.
Chaw la gyap su chio.
I take refuge in Dharma.

Sangham sharanam gacchami.
Gendun la gyap su chio.
I take refuge in the spiritual community.

In Tibet, the teacher is considered most important, because it is the lama who embodies and makes the Three Jewels accessible. Thus, the line, "lama la gyap su chio [I take refuge in the teacher]" is added at the beginning. The short form of the bodhisattva's refuge vow is, "I take refuge in the Three Jewels until I reach the core of enlightenment in order to help other beings."

The Sanskrit term *sharanam gacchami* means to seek shelter or protection, as explained in *The Crown of Great Vehicle Sutras*:

> From all personal harm and destruction,
> From the lesser vehicle and lack of method,
> And from lower rebirth it protects,
> Thus it is the holy refuge.

Taking Refuge

The act of taking refuge is either mundane or transcendent. The mundane is determined by attitude or type of refuge object. The transcendent is either common or unique, the common being that of the disciples and solitary buddhas and the unique being that of the great vehicle or the tantric vehicle. The common motive in mundane refuge taking are fear [of misery, death, and lower rebirth] and desire [for personal welfare]. The disciples and solitary buddhas are also motivated by fear and desire, but their main motivation is faith. Bodhisattvas may also have these motivations, but their main motive is *compassion*.

Mundane refuge objects are either inferior, like the gods Ishvara and Brahma, mountains, trees, and the like, or superior, which means taking refuge in the Three Jewels with the mundane motive of protection from fear or desire for good things. Taking refuge in the Three Jewels with mundane motivation will never lead to freedom from samsara.

The objectives of transcendent refuge are either common or unique. The two common types are the disciples' refuge in the Three Jewels mainly out of desire for involvement in the community of monks, and the solitary buddhas' mainly for Dharma. Of the unique types, followers of the transcendence (great) vehicle

take refuge in the Three Jewels mainly for Buddha, as explained in
The Peerless Principle:

> To be free of delusion
> To be free of fear
> Neither Dharma nor noble community
> Are ultimate refuge objects.
> For those who would be holy
> Buddha is the only refuge.

The way of taking refuge of the tantric vehicle is a subject of the
secret teachings, so I won't go into it here. **[2.A]**

Mundane refuge is taken simply for personal advancement and
welfare in present and future lives, not "until the core of enlightenment" or "for the duration of lives." Disciples and solitary buddhas
take refuge for the duration of lives, but not "until the core of
enlightenment." Bodhisattvas take refuge until they attain enlightenment; they accept nothing else.

Concerning the goal, ordinary people take refuge as though it
were an escort to their goal of personal welfare in present and
future lives. Disciples take refuge to attain arhatship for themselves, and solitary buddhas to obtain the state of unconditional
awareness for themselves, even without the teachings of a Buddha,
through realization of dependent occurrence [on their own].
Bodhisattvas wish to attain the omniscience of buddhahood in
order to help other beings.

How to Take Refuge

General Instructions

The general instructions deal with what to accomplish and what
to avoid. What to accomplish consists of associating with spiritual
persons, learning holy Dharma, and practicing it. After learning
Dharma from a qualified teacher, you should place confidence in
friends who are spiritually developed and introduce relatives and
friends to Dharma. You should attend to the teachings in the three

divisions of canonical scriptures, which are the actual words of Buddha or, if you have the empowerment, attend to the four classes of tantra.[2] In addition, you should study the texts [*śastra*] elucidating the Buddha's intentions composed by Maitreya, Asaṅga and his brother Vasubandhu, Nāgārjuna and his disciple Āryadeva, Dignāga, Dharmakīrti, Candrakīrti, Śāntideva, Guṇaprabha, and so on. For the secret teachings you should study *The Three Bodhisattva Commentaries*, *The Seven Volumes on Siddhis* by the [Indian] siddhas, and the works of the yogins Virlapa, Rāja Indrabhūti, Vajraghanta, and others.

In brief, you should listen, study, meditate, and practice the teachings spoken by Buddha, compiled by his disciples, the "collectors," practiced by the siddhas, explained by the great scholars [*acaryā*], translated by qualified translators, and taught by skillful teachers. Any other teaching, though seeming to be profound, is not true buddha dharma and not fit to be heard, studied, meditated, or practiced. False dharma, no matter how attractive, should be rejected.

Practicing dharma means behaving according to the scriptures and specific practices in the course of daily activities. Your behavior should be in accord with the discipline scriptures [*vinaya*], your meditation with the sutra scriptures, your knowledge with the illuminating science scriptures [*abhidharma*], and your understanding of the secret teachings with the tantras. These days I've seen a lot of strange "dharma" that doesn't agree with the foregoing—I don't know *what* it is!

Specific practices in the course of daily activities are as follows: When staying somewhere, think of the Three Jewels as your support. When traveling, think of them situated in the place you're headed, as though you're approaching them for refuge. After arriving, visualize Vairocana Buddha at that spot, Akṣobhya to the east, Ratnasambhava to the south, Amitābha to the west, and Amoghasiddhi to the north, and pray that hindrances be removed, your goals be achieved, and that you'll eventually take

---

[2]Action (*kriyātantra*), behavior (*caryātantra*), identity (*yogatantra*), and supreme identity (*anutaratantra*). See Herbert Guenther, *Buddhist Philosophy in Theory and Practice* (Berkeley: Shambhala, 1971).

your place among the buddhas. When eating, offer the first portion to your teacher, reciting the mantra "Oṃ Mahāguru Vajra Naividyā. Āḥ Hūṃ" as indicated in many sutras and tantras including the *Vajra Tip* and *Wheel of Time* tantras. In addition, it is also good to make general food offerings to all buddhas, bodhisattvas and personal deities, reciting, "Oṃ Sarva Buddha Bodhisattva Vajra Naividyā. Āḥ Hūṃ." Offerings of water must be pure and unmixed with food.

In the yoga of food, you should eat only as much as you need. In the yoga of sleep, go to sleep thinking that it is like the Buddha's final nirvana [death]. Lie on your right side with head to the east or north, and after becoming focused in concentration on Amiābha, sleep absorbed in the voidness of buddha's reality body. When getting up, rise with the "pride" [3] of buddha's form body. Perform all daily activities according to *The Purification of the Environment Sutra*. Offer your pleasures and happiness to your teacher and the Three Jewels, and if you have any illness or misery, don't lose faith in them. Since medical treatment, curative rituals, visualizations and prayers are all branches of the Dharma jewel, be careful not to abuse them. In short, practice devotion to the Three Jewels in all activities, and don't lose faith even in the face of death. [2.B]

Specific Instructions

Concerning specific instructions *The Crown of Great Vehicle Sutras* states:

> One who takes refuge in Buddha
> Is a true devotee [*upāsaka*],
> And never goes for refuge
> To other "deities."
> After taking refuge in holy Dharma
> Eliminate harmful intentions and killing,

---

[3]In this case pride refers to the tantric practice of identification with a buddha or personal diety (*yidam*). For an explanation of the "bodies" of a buddha, see Chapter 8.

> After taking refuge in the spiritual community
> Don't associate with the unspiritual.

If you've taken refuge in Buddha, don't consider anyone else as the ultimate teacher. If you've taken refuge in Dharma, don't harm any living being or behave in any way not in harmony with Dharma. If you've taken refuge in the spiritual community, don't take a nonbuddhist as a real teacher or associate frequently with people outside the community, or stay at their places of worship. You won't harm your refuge just by paying respects or making offerings to mundane deities like the dharma protectors or local deities, but if you think of them as *ultimate* refuge you'll break your refuge vow. It's like a citizen of one country offering respect to the ruler of another; it doesn't make him a traitor. But if he asks the ruler of another country for refuge, he has defected from his former ruler's domain. Calling another deity "Lord" is harmful to your refuge in Buddha.

Failure to pay proper respect to Dharma because of preoccupation with business affairs or neglecting to listen and study, thinking it won't actually harm your refuge, is called "backsliding in Dharma refuge." Business involvements often affect Dharma refuge and can even ruin it. Those who disrespect the yellow robe [of monks] will lose their refuge in the community. Slight or unintentional disrespect won't ruin your refuge, but great disrespect or intentional harm to monks or great teachers will. I would say more about this, but you should look up the specific instructions in the sutra literature.

The Benefits of Taking Refuge

The benefits of following these instructions are temporal benefits of freedom and spiritual development, and final benefits for yourself and others. The temporal benefits of freedom are reduction of the hindrance of behavior based on wrong beliefs, deflection of harm from humans and natural forces, and fewer physical and mental problems. There is said to be some benefit from simply reciting the refuge formula, not even from the depths of your heart.

The story of the senile monk is a good example. **[2.C]** There are also the temporal benefits of the spiritual assets of being considered a spiritual person, obtaining superior positions in the world's higher realms, being protected by beneficial forces in general, and in particular by the great dharma protectors who guard the teachings, having a guide who is like the leader of a great expedition, and happiness in this life and the assurance of not losing the Three Jewels in future lives.

The final benefits are that refuge in Buddha leads to perfect buddhahood, refuge in Dharma enables you to turn the wheel of Dharma, and refuge in community provides the good fortune of membership in the community of monks and bodhisattvas. The benefit for others is that, inspired by your own achievement, other people will become involved in correct practice and eventually achieve the final benefits for themselves.

3

The Intent
for Enlightenment

The intent for enlightenment is the dedication to attain enlightenment in order to help others do likewise. There are two
types, relative and absolute. The relative intent is compassion for
unliberated beings and the absolute intent is the experiential
realization that all beings and things are naturally void of inherent, independent existence. Although the two seem contradictory, they must be unified during the final phase of practice. That
is, at the very moment of experiencing the voidness of persons or
things, the relative intent of compassion toward beings must be
retained. [4]

Generally speaking, the relative intent is produced through
[causal conditions such as] ritual, whereas the absolute intent is
not. The relative intent is produced through causal factors indicated by concepts transmitted through the teachings of the
masters, whereas the absolute intent is not produced directly from
causal factors because it involves unconditioned gnosis. Even the
conventional expression "production of absolute intent" does not
accord with the views of the masters. What is loosely called

---

[4] See *The Door of Liberation.* (Novato, CA: Lotsawa, 1988) pp. 87-89.

"production of absolute intent" is attained upon perception of the voidness of phenomena on the insight path, which follows [but is not "produced" by] the final phase of the application path, which *is* produced through the strength of the accumulations of merit and wisdom. In short, the relative intent is produced through the teachings of others, whereas the absolute intent is a purely subjective experience.

Both lesser and greater vehicles have systems for producing the intent for enlightenment. **3.A** I will outline the basic Middle Way system for producing the aspirational and functional relative intent. [More specific instructions for actual practice are given in section 4.5.]

Instructions for the Aspirational Intent

The aspirational intent for enlightenment is basically the intention to attain buddhahood in order to help other beings. The instructions for producing the aspirational intent deal with its principal causes, conditions that strengthen it, and methods for preventing its degeneration.[5]

The principal causes of the aspirational intent are compassion and love, which are essentially the desire that you and all other beings be free from misery and have happiness [and are instigated by the miseries of samsara], as indicated in *The Crown of Great Vehicle Sutras*: "The rivers of compassion and love truly spring from misery itself." Strive to develop compassion and love through the practices explained in section 4.5.2.

There are seven conditions that strengthen the aspirational intent: reliance on a true spiritual friend (teacher), strong devotion toward and reasonable faith in the Three Jewels, recognizing and eliminating evil behavior as explained in the sutras, praying to all buddhas and bodhisattvas that you will not be tempted to act improperly, reflecting on the advantages of the intent for en-

---

[5]The following two paragraphs have been moved forward in the text for clarity.

lightenment and the disadvantages of samsara and the two nirvanas,[6] recalling the spiritual assets of buddhas and bodhisattvas
such as the ability to produce physical emanations, clairvoyance,
and the like [see Chapter 8], and enthusiasm for working for the
welfare for yourself and others. To cultivate these conditions,
produce a sincere desire to confess and correct improper behavior
by understanding the disadvantages of samsara, correct infatua-
tion with [the experience of] extreme voidness by understanding
the disadvantages of the two types of nirvana, prevent despair at
[the misery of] samsara by envisioning the fulfillment of the great
purpose of human existence, be inspired about the temporal and
final results [of practice] by imagining the spiritual assets of
buddhas and bodhisattvas, pray to your teacher and the Three
Jewels that you not yield to evil behavior, and quickly receive the
blessings to become a bodhisattva. These practices will strengthen
the intent by increasing conducive conditions and reducing
obstructions. **3.B**

Concerning the methods for preventing degeneration of the
aspirational intent, negative attitudes and lack of sincere respect
for your teacher and the Three Jewels will cause degeneration of
your intent. Favoring your own happiness and interests over others
or jealousy at another person's good fortune or accomplishments
will cause degeneration. Other causes of degeneration are neglecting to practice with correct methods because of the belief that
"recognition of mind-in-itself" is sufficient [see section 4.6.2.1],
and not knowing the spiritual assets of buddhas and bodhisattvas
and thus not striving to gain them for yourself. The antidote is

---

[6]This refers to the goal of practice of the lesser vehicle: the nirvana without
residue, which is total and final cessation of personal existence, and the nirvana
with residue, which is a temporary cessation of existence caused by the failure to
eliminate slight residual karmic elements that result in rebirth into worldly
existence after many eons. In the great vehicle, these nirvanas are considered
undesirable dead ends, although the nirvana with residue is sometimes appropriate for persons who are unable to deal with the pain of samsara. On the other
hand, adherents of the lesser vehicle feel that the lofty ideals of the great vehicle
and its goal of complete, perfect enlightenment are impossible for anyone except
the one Buddha of each eon, who in our eon was the historical person
Śākyamuni.

cultivation of [the seven conditions that strengthen intent], such as devotion, inspiration and so on, as described before.

Further, you should know the three main causes of failure and the antidotes. First, discouragement can cause failure to apply yourself in practice, feeling that someone like yourself couldn't possibly accomplish the difficult task of attaining buddhahood. The antidote for this is self-encouragement:

Why were we born as human beings?
In any moment of immeasurable time
You can attain perfect enlightenment,
So don't give in to discouragement. (CS)

You were born as a human
Able to tell good from bad;
If you devote yourself to practice
Why wouldn't you attain enlightenment? (EBP)

A good example is the story of the brahmin's daughter who gave the Buddha a bowl of rice. Buddha told her that by the merit of her gift she would be reborn in higher realms in all future lives and finally attain buddhahood. Her husband said, "Gautama, having renounced a kingdom, tells lies for a bowl of rice!" So Muni asked him, "How big was the seed that produced the huge tree by your doorway?" Muni responded, "Then *you* must be lying," and on hearing this the man saw the truth [and became an arhat]. *The Good Eon Sutra* [Bhadrakalpika] states that the intent for enlightenment can be produced and buddhahood eventually attained merely through offerings of spice, a blade of grass, or even a piece of dung. Since mental attitude is the essential factor, you can even offer the unofferable—the universe itself, as in this prayer by Śāntideva:

Whatever flowers and fruits there are,
Whatever kinds of medicine,
Whatever is precious in this world,
And all its pure refreshing waters.

Mountains of gems, and yes,
The forests of solitary, peaceful joy,
Trees brilliantly adorned with blossoms,
Or branches bent with fine fruit.

Lakes and ponds adorned with lotus,
Wild geese filling the sky
With cries so beautiful—
Everything unpossessable in this vast universe.

Holding all this in mind, I offer it
To Muni and his offspring;
With pure and great compassion for me
Kindly accept this gift.

I am poor and have no wealth,
I've nothing else to offer,
So you with kind intent for others,
Accept this for my sake also. (EBP)

Second, some people foolishly fail to cultivate the intent because they are worried that the results of practice might not occur in the present life. Like practicing generosity but still being poor, practicing morality but still being sickly, or performing curative rituals and reciting prayers but still losing the patient. The feeling that those things were ineffectual is a disappointment, and its antidote is cultivation of a positive attitude. 3.C

You should also understand some things about action [karma] and its result. Action can produce results in the present life, in the next life, or after a number of rebirths. To produce results in the present life, exceptionally significant intent, action, and object of action must be involved. Such actions are extremely rare, and anything less will not produce results until the next life or after several rebirths. Thus, a person might behave badly and not strive for happiness, yet experience happiness in the present life. The opposite can also happen. This is a sign that the results of a person's actions will be experienced in future lives. Thus it is extremely hard to understand the cause-and-effect relationship of action.

Third, failure to produce the intent can be caused by over-whelming despair at the miseries of birth, sickness, old age and death, or by repulsion at atrocities committed by especially evil persons, or by the exhaustion of having wandered in samsara for a very long time. These can be corrected, respectively, by realizing that the compulsive aggregates [which compose the body and mind] are illusory, by striving to think of all beings as if they were an only child, and by realizing that since the past, present and future are actually timeless, there's no difference between an eon and an instant. It also helps to think about your teacher in order to strengthen the impulse for the intent through recalling his example.

Instructions for Producing the Functional Intent

[The aspirational intent
And functional intent
Are like someone wanting to travel
And a traveler on a journey.
The aspirational intent for enlightenment
Produces great benefits even in samsara,
But cannot compare with the functional intent
Which pours out benefits ceaselessly. (EBP)]

To produce the functional intent, you should try to avoid improper actions and cultivate virtuous behavior according to your ability. If improper actions are inadvertently done, confess in the evening what you did that day and confess the next day what you did the previous night.[7] Dedicate every spiritual quality you've developed, no matter how small, to accomplishing the welfare of all beings. Nāgārjuna's *Friendly Letter to the King* is especially relevant for lay practictioners:

---

[7]This refers to the formal practice of confession between fellow monks or nuns. Laypersons can confess as soon as possible directly to their teacher, or mentally to their teacher or Buddha. When doing this it is essential to have sincere regret but not guilt, which will hinder the practice.

Great King, you have much work and many responsibilities, and no time day or night to practice the six transcendences, from giving to wisdom. Therefore, you should practice by having faith in real, perfect enlightenment, and always remember to aspire and strive to help others in all your affairs. Rejoice in the merits of others and offer this unselfish joy to all buddhas, bodhisattvas, disciples, and solitary buddhas. Work earnestly together with everyone, with the intention of attaining peerless enlightenment on the same day that every other being perfects their own spiritual qualities. Great King, if you do this your royal responsibilities and affairs of state will not be affected, and you will also complete the accumulation of merit and wisdom which are needed to attain enlightenment. **3.D**

The formal instructions for the functional intent deal with the causes of production, conditions for strengthening it, and methods for preventing degeneration. The functional intent is cultivated after the aspirational intent is produced and developed through the methods for strengthening and preventing degeneration. Then, while continuing to meditate on the miseries of samsara and the disadvantages of the nirvana of the lesser vehicle, work to quickly liberate all beings from samsara, but avoid nirvana as if it were poisoned food. Conditions that strengthen the functional intent are meditative recollection of buddhas, bodhisattvas and teachers, and performance of the seven-part worship three times each day and night. **3.E** To prevent its degeneration, learn the various ways to repair lapses and improper behavior, such as the Hundred Syllable Mantra of the Tathagatas **3.F**, the antidotes for major lapses explained in *The Space Womb Sutra*, and the antidotes for major and minor lapses from *The Heap of Jewels Sutra*.

[Santideva expressed the essence of the intent for enlightenment with exceptional eloquence in these verses added from the third chapter of *Entering the Bodhisattva's Practice*:

For those who are sick
May I be doctor, medicine

And attendant,
Till health is restored.

For the poor may I be a treasury,
Inexhaustible for the giving.
May I live among them
Providing the necessities of life.

My body, its pleasures,
And any merit I've gained
I'll give without second thought
To help other beings.

I offer my body to others
For whatever be their pleasure.
Let them despise, strike,
Even murder—whatever they please,
Let them play with my body!
Let it be the object of laughter and scorn!

But let no harm come to them
For anything they do.
May anything they do to me
Always result in benefit to them.

Whatever they feel, hatred or trust,
From their attitude toward me—
May it always result in achievement
Of all their goals.

May whoever accuses me,
Or curses me
Or insults me,
All have the fortune of enlightenment.

I'll be protection for the unprotected,
A guide for those on a journey,
And for those wishing to cross over—
A boat, a ship, or a bridge.

May I be a garden for gardeners
A bed for those needing a bed,
And a slave
For anyone wanting a slave.

May I be the source of nourishment
For every life-form in the universe
Stretching to the limits of space
Till they achieve freedom from misery.

Today my life is fruitful,
My human existence well taken.
Today I was born into the family of buddhas;
A child of the buddhas I've become today.

Like a blind man finding a jewel
In a heap of garbage,
Through what good fortune
Was this intent born in me?

This is the supreme antidote
That conquers mankind's Lord of Death,
The inexhaustible treasure
That removes mankind's poverty.

This is the best medicine
For mankind's sickness
Miraculous tree relieving the fatigue
Of exhausted wanderers in samsara.

It's the bridge of all mankind
For escape from lower existence,
The great sun that clears away
The mists of mankind's ignorance.

For wanderers on the paths of samsara
Craving the experience of bliss,
It is the source of highest bliss—
A feast granting complete satisfaction.

Today in the presence of the protectors,
I invite all beings to this joyful feast
Till they attain enlightenment.
May everyone in the world rejoice!]

4

The Six Transcendences

The six transcendences are practiced primarily to develop your own spiritual qualities. They constitute an integrated set of methods for transcending ["passing beyond"] *both samsara and nirvana*, the individual transcendences being the specific practices for attaining enlightenment. They are called giving, morality, patience, effort, meditative absorption, and wisdom.

The transcendences are six in number because they provide six necessary things for achieving your own and others' welfare. From giving you obtain the necessities of life, from morality, a healthy body in good circumstances, patience results in good companions, effort yields success in all activities, meditative absorption suppresses emotional afflictions, and wisdom yields undeludedness in all activities. Nothing more is needed and anything less is insufficient. Giving and patience are especially relevant for lay practictioners, morality and absorption for monks, and effort and wisdom for both. This is because laypersons have possessions and competitors, and thus more need to practice giving and patience than monks, who have few possessions and enemies. It is easier for monks to practice morality and absorption because they've renounced distracting circumstances and live in isolated places, whereas lay persons, even when keeping vows of temporary abstinence and not killing, have many obstacles to morality, and the distractions of household activities and family make it difficult to focus the mind in concentration. Effort and wisdom are important for both, for they provide incentive for practice and understanding of the nature of things.

The order of the six transcendences is based on three factors. The first is sequential dependence: when not obsessed with possessions you can practice morality, when maintaining the morality of vows you can be patient with those who harm you, when you have patience you can increase your effort, with increased effort concentration can be achieved, and when you can focus your mind in equanimity you can realize the true nature of things. Second, they are ordered from lower to higher, giving being lower than morality, and so on up to wisdom. Third, they progress from simpler to subtler: giving is the simplest and easiest to practice, whereas morality is more subtle and difficult, and so on up to wisdom, the most difficult and subtle. The transcendences should be practiced in an integrated manner, however:

> [Practice the six transcendences
> With awareness of their relative importance.
> Don't sacrifice the greater for the lesser;
> Weight the importance of each against the others. (EBP)]

Giving

Giving means using something of value to help others. When developed along with preparation, actual realization states, and postrealization practice [of wisdom],[8] it becomes transcendant

---

[8]Each experiential realization of voidness through wisdom involves three phases. In the preparation phase, which is mundane, effort is made to analyze the objective, such as the egolessness of persons or the identitylessness of things. The actual realization state, which is transcendent, consists of the experiential realization of voidness during which the apparent nature of things is not perceived. The postrealization phase is again mundane but is influenced by the preceding realization state. The unification of actual realization and postrealization states, the goal of advanced meditation, permits the simultaneous perception of both the apparent aspect and ultimate voidness of phenomena. See

giving. To understand the nature of giving you must know its antithesis, the antidotes, and correct accomplishment.

The Antithesis of Giving

The antithesis of giving is selfishness, which inhibits generosity; or, if not completely inhibiting it, taints it with ulterior motives; or, even if not tainting it, prevents it from being conducive to enlightenment. The fault of selfishness in this life is that everyone dislikes a self-centered person. Consider the meaning of these verses by Āryadeva:

> A fool experiences the misery of hoarding
> And never the happiness of practice;
> Constantly in search of profit—
> A miser's wealth is like a packrat's.
>
> Possessions gotten in time of need
> Are like a gift, Muni said;
> But hoarded wealth's like honey—
> Eventually consumed by others.

Selfishness also destroys happiness in future lives, for the miserly are reborn as frustrated spirits or as humans in impoverished circumstances.

Types of Giving

The cause of selfishness is attachment to material possessions, and the antidote is to learn generosity. There are three categories of

---

section 4.6 on transcendent wisdom for a more detailed discussion. The import of this statement, repeated for each of the six perfections, is that the practice of giving, morality, and the like is not transcendent until some experience of voidness is achieved through cultivation of wisdom.

giving: that of ordained monks and nuns, that of laypersons, and that of persons who have attained tolerance toward birthlessness.

A monk's gifts are mainly those of fearlessness through example, love, and the teaching of Dharma. His or her material gifts should be simple things like ink, pens, and paper. Not things of great value. A monk who indulges in giving expensive gifts may hinder learning, reflecting and meditating.[9] A monk who cultivates morality, meditative absorption, and wisdom, without being attached to possessions or excessive gift giving, is in harmony with Buddha's teachings.

The sutras say that a monk should give merely the excess from his begging bowl; they do not mention anything else. A monk should be respected by everyone—even the gods—but not as a patron.

Laypersons should first learn to give small gifts to correct any incapacity to give; then, when able to give, they should learn pure giving to correct impure giving; and then learn pure giving that is conducive to buddhahood to correct what is not conducive.

> Gifts of vegetables and such
> Should be made as a start.
> Later, when accustomed to that,
> Giving your own flesh becomes possible.
>
> Then, if you consider your own body
> No different than vegetables,
> How can giving even your flesh
> Be considered difficult? (EBP)

Those who are able to give should learn pure giving to correct impure giving. Some people can't distinguish pure giving from

---

[9]This is the frequently mentioned triad of learning, reflecting, and meditating. Learning (literally, "listening") is study of the teachings concerning the ultimate nature of things—voidness—through books or oral teachings. Reflection is deep and is accomplished through intellectual examination of what was learned. Meditation here denotes the subsequent attempt at transcendent realization of voidness by means of wisdom.

impure giving, which leads them into samsara and lower births. This is very common.

The Sutra Requested by the Rishi rGyas pa mentions thirty types of impure gifts and impure reasons for giving: giving with wrong views, without faith, expecting a return, for protection against fire or flood, out of fear, to please or attract friends, for praise, to cure illness, as a reproach, by an old person to regain youth, to gain fame in another country, to show off, to get a woman, to cure infertility, to be wealthy in future lives; giving to fortunetellers, astrologers, storytellers, doctors, the undeserving, those rich in possessions; giving poison, weapons, slaughtered meat, intoxicating drink, others' possessions, others' food, and necessities to the sick or dying. As the sutra says, abandon them.

There are those who give purely, yet it is not conducive to buddhahood. Some virtues lead to superior existence in the highest realms of gods and human beings, whereas others lead to the nirvana of the disciples and solitary buddhas. Avoiding the trap of nirvana is done by skill in methods, and the pitfall of samsara is avoided by wisdom. Practice with intense effort so that all gifts, however small, are conducive to buddhahood.

The Method of Practicing Pure Giving

Practice in thought. Practice in thought is the cultivation of generous feelings, like joy at seeing a beggar because it is an opportunity to practice giving; or because you can plant the seed for benefits in future lives; or you think of the beggar as an embodiment of the Buddha or a bodhisattva, or that they will be pleased by your giving; or think that you will set an example for the world, or that you might attract the beggar to Dharma.

Practice in deed. Some people hinder themselves by partiality toward the recipient. Some are able to give to their teacher but not to others. Some give for rituals or sutra readings or to venerate the community. Some are able to give only to the poor. Do for now whatever you can to correct this, and gradually learn to extend your generosity.

Practice of time. If you are not ready to give at all times but only on holidays, continue giving at such times, but gradually extend it to other times. The way to do this is to practice generosity for half a day at first. When accustomed to this extend it to a full day, then one month, one year and so on.

Practice of gift. As you give a bottle of water, vegetables, a morsel of food or a fragment of cloth, think, "Although this is insignificant, it is a great gift because, by means of it I may attain buddhahood." Pray that in the future you will be able to give all beings whatever they need. It is better to give a bottle of water than nothing at all. In essence, when you reduce your own arrogance toward others, you won't hinder them; but you will rejoice in their achievements and this will strengthen your intent for enlightenment.

Giving by Those Who Have Attained Tolerance to Birthlessness.[10] Persons who have become tolerant to birthlessness are able to give their domain, members of their family (husband, wife or children), to one who needs them; they can even give their own flesh.

In *The Birth Stories* Buddha, as King Visvantara, gave his wife and children to be servants of a brahmin; as King Sipipa, he gave his eyes to a blind man; and, as a rabbit, he gave his body to a starving brahmin. You should reflect on the meaning of such sutra passages and teach them to others, but, as the sutra says:

> Giving food to the hungry, and clothes, medicine, garlands and money to those who need them is essentially a mental practice. Until you have attained tolerance toward birthlessness, do not give your head, feet, hands or other flesh, even if you are willing.

---

[10]Tolerance to birthlessness denotes the tolerance state that must precede each direct perception of voidness. It is a mental state cleared of obstacles, anxieties, and misconceptions concerning the experience of transcendence, which follows immediately.

And from *Entering the Bodhisattva's Practice*:

> Before compassion is fully perfect
> Do not give your body itself.
> How could that be conducive
> To the welfare of self and others?

To achieve correct giving you must eliminate selfishness, attain unconditioned gnosis, which is the realization of the egolessness of persons and the identitylessness of things, be able to give what is needed in accord with Dharma and assist the development of others, attracting them by giving and then involving them in one of the three vehicles according to their dispositions.

Correct giving also requires the elimination of attachment to material pleasures, procrastination, complacency in giving, expectation of return, expectation of results, latent selfishness, and misdirection. Misdirection is of two types: attraction to the lesser vehicle and belief in the three concepts [the giver, the recipient, and the gift itself].

The Benefits of Giving

The temporal benefits in the present life from pleasing others by giving are obtaining creature comforts, reputation, fame, success, and happiness.

> Though the giver has no desire for comforts
> He gets many material pleasures.

The temporal pleasures of future lives are experiential results, the acquisition of creature comforts, and functional results, the ability to give to others. There are many other benefits, such as never being born in a bad country or in time of famine.

The final benefit is the flowing together of the mundane and transcendent into buddhahood as into an ocean. The holy achievements arise from twin roots of mundane and transcendent virtue, and also from innumerable assets such as the ability for space treasury concentration.

Morality

Morality is avoidance of improper behavior for the sake of others. When developed along with preparation, actual realization states, and postrealization practice, it becomes transcendent morality. To understand moral practice, you must know its antithesis, the antidotes, and correct accomplishment.

The Antithesis of Morality

The antithesis of morality is corrupt moral conduct that hinders you from keeping your commitments; or, if they are kept, you still miss the point the way nonbuddhist moral systems do; or, even if your moral system is correct, it is like the morality of the disciples and not conducive to buddhahood.

The fault of this in the present life is that a person who shows improper moral conduct is despised by everyone. He is ashamed to be with the teacher, associate with the community, or accept gifts from faithful donors. People won't respect him, and all kinds of obstructions to practice will arise. The guardians of Dharma and the meditation deities will not protect him.

Also, your happiness in future lives will be destroyed, for improper behavior does not lead to a happy rebirth. Even minor moral lapses can lead to lower rebirth, and even if a person who is immoral is eventually reborn to a higher existence, unfavorable conditions such as a short life will be inevitable. The scriptures state that killing results in a short life, stealing in loss of wealth, sexual misconduct produces enemies, and lying gives rise to slander. Because of envy, one's hopes will go unrealized, and destructive attitudes will produce misery in a later life.

The Antidotes
to Improper Moral Conduct

Improper moral conduct results from strong negative attitudes and emotions. The provisional antidote is to suppress them, as explained in *The Tantra Requested by Subahu*:

> Correct intense desire by viewing the body
> As unclean flesh, fat, skin, and bones,
> Correct hatred by the river of love,
> Correct delusion by realizing the dependent nature of
>   things,
> And correct pride by realizing one's insignificance in the
>   world.

The conclusive antidote is given by Dharmakīrti in *The Exposition of Valid Knowledge*: "The aim of all meditation is to be liberated by seeing voidness." Master Aryadeva said:

> Elimination of ignorance through wisdom
> Is the real meditation.
> Whatever is eliminated
> Will not reoccur.

Therefore you should become thoroughly practiced in voidness meditation [see sections 4.6 and 6.4].

Through the influence of negative attitudes and emotions your thinking becomes misdirected, resulting in improper physical and verbal behavior. The antidote for this is moral practice. There are three types: practicing vows, developing spiritual assets, and working for the welfare of others. The moral practice of vows includes the Vow of Personal Liberation and Bodhisattva.[11]

---

[11]The vow of personal liberation (*prātimokṣa*) is the commitment of the ordained monk or nun (*bhikṣu, bhikṣuṇī*) to achieve his own liberation. The bodhisattva vow is the commitment to attain buddhahood to help other beings. The vow of personal liberation differs slightly for the monk-bodhisattva and lay-bodhisattva.

The layperson is instructed to take refuge in the Three Jewels, thus becoming a lay devotee [*upāsaka*], maintaining the threefold refuge and observing temporary periods of abstinence [*upavasa*].[12] Then by graded steps, take the first vow of not killing, the second vow of not stealing, the third vow of not lying and, finally, the fourth and fifth vows to abandon sexual misconduct and drinking. The scriptures say that "to practice the ten virtues nothing is needed other than the five vows of the lay devotee." You might wonder how maintaining the five devotee's vows could eliminate the ten vices and cultivate the ten virtues.[13] By keeping the five vows, you will indirectly cultivate the ten virtues. Destructive attitudes are indirectly removed by abandoning killing. Covetousness is indirectly removed by abandoning stealing. Slander and senseless speech are stopped indirectly by abandonment of lying. Wrong views are indirectly removed by the devotee's conviction about the cause-and-effect relationship of action [karma] and its results. Therefore, although the fundamental practice of a lay devotee is cultivation of the ten virtues, they are simplified into five basic precepts for beginners.

The instructions for both novices and fully ordained monks [*bhikṣu*] should be learned from the discipline scriptures [*vinaya*].

When the vow of personal liberation is not accompanied by intent for enlightenment and the purification of the three concepts [of object, action, and recipient of action], it is a lesser vehicle vow; but when it is accompanied, it is the vow of individual liberation of a bodhisattva acting for the sake of others.

The particular practices of the bodhisattva vow are learned *after* producing the intent for enlightenment. In general, the four negative behaviors are to be eliminated and the four positive behaviors cultivated as explained before [Chapter 3].

---

[12]The eightfold vow of temporary abstinence consists of the fivefold vow to abandon killing, stealing, sexual misconduct, lying, and intoxicants, plus the abandonment of music and jewelry, a high seat or bed, and eating after noon.

[13]The ten vices are killing, stealing, sexual misconduct, lying, slander, senseless talking, abusive speech, covetousness, destructive attitudes, and wrong views, such as disbelief in the cause-and-effect relationship of action (karma) or denial of the possibility of liberation.

There are instructions involving the objective field, time, and specific action. In the objective field, abandon the ten vices. First avoid killing yourself and your friends; then extend this to other people and animals. Similarly, learn not to steal from neighbors and relatives, and then extend this to others. The abandonment of lying and the other vices should also be learned by this method of gradual extension.

With regard to time, first get used to avoiding a given vice for half a day, then a full day and night, a week, a month, a year and so on.

As to specific vices, first abandon whichever one you can, and then include a second, a third, and so on, until all ten are abandoned. Start with the gross faults, then the middle ones, and so on until you have eliminated the most subtle.

If a fault occurs, remedy it at once. Don't wait for a more suitable occasion. My own lama, Sakya Chenpo,[14] said, "As a great ocean won't allow a corpse to stay, a spiritual aspirant must not abide lapses."

Before going to sleep, recall whether or not any lapses occurred that day. If none occurred, meditate with joy and dedicate the virtue to buddhahood. If any did occur, confess them at once with sincere regret.

Moral practice for gaining spiritual assets consists of persistent elimination of vices along with their causes. Develop spiritual assets gradually, beginning with taking refuge and working up to the virtues of a buddha. *The Precious Treasury* says:

Learn a word each day
From some important text
And like an anthill or like honey,
You will soon become accomplished.

---

[14]This "Great Sakya" is Jetsun Dakpa Gyentsen (rJe-btsun Drag-pa rgyan-mtsan), the fifth patriarch of the Sakya Order. He was the foremost of Sakya Pandita's Tibetan teachers, and from him Jetsun learned the special doctrines and methods of the Sakya tradition.

Moral practice for the sake of others' welfare means continual attention to eliminating negative things and their causes in order to benefit others most effectively. In working for others' welfare, you may even commit the four destructive acts that are prohibited by your moral vows.

Correct Morality

To achieve correct morality, you must remove corrupt morality, its antithesis; develop preconceptionless realization of egolessness; fulfill your needs by committing body, speech, and mind to morality; and attract other beings with morality and involve them in one of the three vehicles according to their dispositions.

Correct morality also means removing attachment to corrupt morality, procrastination, complacency, expectation of return, expectation of results, latent immorality, and misdirection, which is of two types: abandoning the bodhisattva's vow and belief in the three concepts as mentioned before.

The temporal benefits in the present life from proper moral conduct, happiness and tranquility are having no regrets, all of which result from ease in cultivating the three wisdoms.

One who meditates voidness, kingly concentration,
Bases it on pure moral conduct,
And constantly contemplates the true nature of things.
Less moral persons, striving incorrectly, won't realize
     voidness. (KC)

The sweet fragrance of morality extends everywhere: it validates the receipt of alms in the city, and it makes you a source of refuge for all the world as well as outstanding and resplendent within the spiritual community.

The temporal benefits in future lives are happy rebirths in which you will have good family, sound body, plenty of creature comforts, wisdom, fame, influence, and a long happy life. Through well-kept morality you will always have these conditions regardless of where you are born.

The final benefit is that when you attain buddhahood you will be reknowned as a "teacher of the world," and because you will be pure, with no ulterior motives in physical, verbal, or mental behavior, others will consider you pleasing to know.

Patience

Patience is lack of agitation when harmed by others. When developed along with preparation, actual realization states, and postrealization practice it becomes transcendent patience. To understand patience, you should know its antithesis, the antidotes, and correct accomplishment.

The Antithesis of Patience

The antithesis of patience is anger or mental agitation at harm done by someone else. The faults of this in the present life are described in *Entering the Bodhisattva's Practice*:

> With an attitude of painful hatred
> You'll have no peace of mind,
> Nor joy or happiness.
> Unable to sleep, you will have no rest.

A hate-filled mind is always unhappy and is unable to rest or sleep comfortably. An irritated, rancorous mind will never be relaxed or healthy; a hate-filled person is not self-directed, but is driven by reactions to others' actions. Hindered in associating with teachers, spiritual friends, and patrons, you will not be happy in spiritual practice. You will never be considered a religious person. Unreligious, bad-natured married couples quarrel all their lives. Not speaking to each other, they force their children to be mediators. Yet after quarreling their whole lives, when one dies, the other grieves. What is the use? You must abandon hatred.

Hatred will also destroy happiness in future lives.

All good deeds—
Giving, worshipping the Sugata—
Compiled over a thousand eons,
Are destroyed by a moment of anger. (EBP)

Your hatred destroys the virtue you have accumulated through many eons, and you will remain unliberated even after many rebirths.

The Antidotes to Lack of Patience

To eliminate hatred you must first remove its cause.

From encountering unpleasant things
Hatred grows, self-destructively.
If the harm is reparable,
Why be upset?
And if it is not,
What good does anger do? (EBP)

When someone dies or a vessel is broken, it is irreparable. What good does it do to be upset? Take joy in recalling this lesson. When your body is wounded or your house is damaged, if it is possible to repair it, displeasure is unnecessary. Slight agitation may occur in one who is free of such displeasure, but actual hatred will not arise.

The antidote to hatred is patience: the patience of accepting the burden of misery, the patience of mental certitude towards things, and patience in the face of harm. Regarding the first, the buddhas and bodhisattvas of former times attained buddhahood through endurance of the miseries of heat, cold, hunger, thirst, sickness, demons, and of other physical, verbal, and mental austerities for the sake of accomplishing spiritual aims, eliminating wrong physical and verbal actions in themselves and others. If in order to achieve buddhahood you might have to endure even the tortures of hell, what can be said of any current misery? Understanding its necessity, meditate on patiently accepting the burden of misery. It says in a sutra:

> When you practice in a desolate place, carnivorous animals may torment you or bandits may harm you. You should think: "May my defilement of action [karma] be purified by this. May no such harm occur in the buddha-field of my buddhahood." Practice the purification of the environment [see next section] and the development of beings in this way.

Practice mental certitude toward things by meditating on superficial and absolute patience. Superficial patience is practiced by considering the harm done to yourself by external things. Samsara is naturally miserable. Fire is naturally hot. Likewise, water is naturally wet, earth hard, air motile, and space empty. As beings are naturally wild, anger toward them is illogical.

> The "malice" of fire is its burning nature;
> Beings are wild like the sky,
> What's the use of destroying them?
> Once the enemy, anger, is destroyed,
> All other enemies flee like robbers. (EBP)

"Aren't beings basically good, their faults just ephemeral?" it might be asked. In this case also, anger is illogical, "like the malice of dust blown through the sky."

To meditate on absolute patience, correct anger by attributing the situation to your own bad karma. Think: "This is the natural result of harm previously done by me to other beings. Why be angry at anyone but myself?"

> Previously I have done
> Such harm to beings,
> It is fitting that this malicious being
> Return that harm to me.

> Thus, if I injure myself with a weapon,
> At whom can I be angry?

Why did I previously commit
Action harmful to others?
Everything depends on action;
What revenge can I take against that?

Harmful beings rise against me
Through the force of my own action.
If I hurl them thus into hell
Won't I have caused their ruination? (EBP)

Correct yourself recalling the total interconnectedness of the phenomenal world.

To meditate on absolute patience when harmed by another, realize that the self that is harmed, the enemy who harms, and the harm itself do not exist in the absolute sense. Anger is extinguished through this doorway of freedom from preconceived attitudes.

Thus, regarding things, which are void,
What can be gained and what lost?
Who performs religious rites,
And what is to be gained?
Who is happy or miserable?
What satisfaction or dissatisfaction can there be?
Likewise, in striving for anything,
Who is attached and to what attached?

On examination, everyone alive
In this world will die;
This is what has been and what will be.
Even friends and relatives, what are they?
Realize that, like yourself,
Everything is like space. (EBP)

The meditation of patience in the face of harm requires the threefold practice of field, time, and nature. Extend the field, cultivating patience initially toward relatives, then friends, and finally enemies. Practice patience for increasing periods of time, beginning with half a day. Take an oath during this time not to think: "I hope no one harms me so I don't have to practice patience."* Then extend this to one whole day, then a day and a night, one fortnight, one month, one year, and so on.

Regarding the nature of the objects of patience, cultivate patience because all beings are really our relatives, our mothers or sons. Learn not to feel hatred at their harmful acts.

If there were no enemy, there would be no occasion to practice patience. When you see an enemy, take joy in thinking: "Now I will perfect my transcendent patience." Moreover, you should cultivate patience because it is a condition for the exhaustion of bad action [karma].

> Without harmful people, patience cannot arise;
> Only when they exist can it arise.
> Because they are its cause,
> How can they be called obstacles?
>
> So if patience is produced
> Through another's hate-filled mind,
> That other is the very cause of patience,
> Fit to be worshipped like Holy Dharma.
>
> Thus, like a treasure found in your house
> Without effort,
> An enemy should be received with joy
> And he is the bodhisattva's friend. (EBP)

Correct Accomplishment of Patience

Correct accomplishment of patience requires the development of four good qualities and the elimination of seven attachments. The four good qualities are removal of anger, which is the antithesis of patience; preconceptionless realization of egolessness; fulfillment

---

*Because the code of discipline prohibits a monk from taking an oath, he should practice patience by a promise in the presence of (symbols of) the Three Jewels—SP.

of others' welfare through the cultivation of patience; and development of other beings, leading to their involvement in the three vehicles. The seven attainments are given in section 4.1.3 on the benefits of giving.

The temporal benefits of cultivating patience that occur in the present life are the immeasurable benefits such as the ability to withstand harm from others without returning it, the resultant pacification of others' harmful intentions and behavior, your own physical and mental happiness deriving from their pacification, present comfort, eventual pacification of all enemies, and fearlessness when departing from this world.

The temporal benefits in future lives are a good body wherever you are born, a long life free from sickness, freedom from human and nonhuman enemies, and the power to obtain preeminence among gods and men.

The final benefit is that, endowed with the thirty-two major signs and eighty minor marks of a great being, you will possess a beautiful body and voice so as to captivate the minds of all beings.

Effort

Effort is inspiration for spiritual practice for the sake of others. When developed along with preparation, actual realization states, and postrealization practice, it becomes transcendent effort. To understand effort you should know its antithesis, its antidotes, and correct accomplishment.

The Antithesis of Effort

The antithesis of effort is complacent laziness, the failure to apply yourself to physical, verbal, and mental practices, or making effort to practice what is not really beneficial, such as nonbuddhist practice, or making effort in beneficial practices but still falling within the limits of samsara and nirvana.

Consider the faults of this in the present life and the destruction of happiness in future lives.

Abandoning effort through discouragement,
And thus impoverished, how will you be liberated?
And making effort with pride
Is a temptation even for a great man. (EBP)

Discouraged and procrastinating out of laziness, you won't even be able to take care of your food, clothing, farming, and other worldly business, to say nothing of beneficial practices such as listening, reflecting, and meditating. How will you meet enlightened persons and their teachings? You will be hindered in practice and even your worldly affairs will deteriorate. This is illustrated by historical cases of rulers who ruined their administrations and commoners who ruined their affairs such as farming and business. In this way you will be despised by everyone.

About the destruction of happiness in future lives, *The Mother of Conquerors* states, "If out of laziness you can't accomplish even your own welfare, what can be said of others' welfare?"

If you've anxiety about this life
When seeing the struggles of a dying fish,
What can be said of the unbearable miseries
Of the hells resulting from evil deeds? (EBP)

The Antidotes to Complacent Laziness

The causes of complacent laziness are given in *Entering the Bodhisattva's Practice*:

Laziness—attraction to the bad,
Disappointment, self-doubt,
Indolence, fondness for happiness,
Addiction to sleep,
Not being upset with samsara's miseries—
These produce complacent laziness.

Laziness, which hinders virtuous work, is the postponing or neglecting of any affairs. It is produced by attraction to bad activities or worldly matters such as business and socializing; by disappointment caused by unfruitfulness of virtuous work, which discourages practice; by self-doubt in which one feels that "a person like myself can't possibly become advanced"; by indolence, which hinders virtuous work through habitual sleeping and lying down; by fondness for the pleasures of eating, drinking, senseless conversation, and other pastimes; by addiction to sleep, which hinders beneficial work through wasted days and nights spent sleeping; and by not being dissatisfied with samsara—failing to realize its inherent miseries of birth, aging, sickness and death.

Concerning the antidotes for the foregoing, the following exhortation is given in *Entering the Bodhisattva's Practice*:

> The afflicted are like fish on a hook;
> After so many rebirths they're caught again
> In the Lord of Death's jaws,
> Yet still don't know his name.

> Gradually killing yourself.
> Do you even see it?
> One so enmeshed in sleep
> Is like butcher and water-buffalo.

> After all paths are blocked,
> The Lord of Death looks at you.
> How can you take pleasure in eating?
> How can you sleep? How can you be happy?

> You'll die too soon,
> Unable to compile the [two] stores.
> When the Lord of Death suddenly comes
> You'll realize, "Alas, it's too late!"

Counter complacency by recalling over and over all the signs of samsara's faults. Further, the specific antidotes of laziness are the practice of purification of the environment and correct accomplishment. The former is explained in *The Purification of the Environment Sutra*, which is contained in *The Buddha Wreath*

Sutra. If you can't understand its wording, study this *Epitome of Purification of the Environment* by Jñānagarbha and practice accordingly:

> When sitting in a house a bodhisattva should think, "May I attain the palace of great liberation." When sleeping, "May I obtain the reality body of Buddha." If dreams occur, "May I realize that all things are like dreams." When waking, "May I awaken from ignorance." When dressing, "I am putting on the garments of conscience and awareness." When tying the sash, "May I fasten the roots of virtue." When sitting on a cushion, "May I attain the adamantine seat, the core of enlightenment." When leaning back, "May I recline in the field of enlightenment." When lighting a fire, "May I burn with the fire of gnosis." When cooking, "May I brew the nectar of gnosis." And when eating, "May I eat the food of the meditative absorptions." When going outside, "May I escape the prison of samsara." When descending stairs, "May I descend into samsara for the sake of beings." When opening a door, "May I open the door to the city of liberation." When closing a door, "May I close the door on the three lower existences." When setting out on a road, "May I embark on the superior path." When traveling upward, "May I establish all beings in the happiness of the higher existences." When descending, "May I break the continuity of the three lower existences." When meeting a being, "May I meet the perfect Buddha." When setting down a foot, "May I support the welfare of all beings." When raising a foot, "May I pull all beings from samsara." Seeing a person adorned with jewelry, "May I wear the ornaments of the [thirty-two] signs and [eighty] marks of a great being." Seeing someone without jewelry, "May I be endowed with the good qualities of purity." Seeing a full vessel, "May I be filled with good qualities." Seeing an empty vessel, "May I be emptied of faults." Seeing many happy people, "May I be happy in Dharma." Seeing someone displeased, "May I be displeased with all synthetic things." Seeing a happy person, "May I obtain the bliss of buddhahood." Seeing a miserable being, "May I allay the misery of all beings." Seeing a sick

person, "May I free all beings from sickness." Seeing an attractive person, "May all beings obtain the attractiveness of buddhas and bodhisattvas." Seeing an ugly person, "May all beings avoid unvirtuous spiritual teachers." Seeing kindness returned, "May I return the kindness of buddhas and bodhisattvas." Seeing kindness unreturned, "May I not return the 'kindness of wrong views.'" Seeing a monk, "May I become involved in superior dharma." Seeing a person practicing austerities, "May I be able to practice the austerities of holy dharma." Seeing an armored person, "May I don armor to seek holy dharma." Seeing an unarmored person, "May I not bear the armoring of nonvirtuous action." Seeing people quarreling, "May I stop all opponents of the correct view." Seeing a person praised, "May all buddhas and bodhisattvas be praised." Seeing a city, "May I see the city of liberation." Seeing a forest, "It is the gathering place for all holy beings." Teaching dharma, "May I never stop learning buddha-dharma." When crossing over water, "May I cross the ocean of samsara." When washing, "May I be cleansed of physical and mental taints." When hot, "May the pain of the afflictions be cooled." When cold, "May I obtain the coolness of nirvana." When reciting dharma, "May I obtain the unclouded vision that sees all buddhas." When seeing a reliquary, "May it be an object of worship for all living beings." When beholding it, "May all beings behold it." When bowing, "May I not be considered anything special by the world." When circumambulating it, "May I be in harmony with the goal of omniscience." When reciting the good qualities of a buddha, "May I encompass all the inexhaustible qualities."

Similarly, when reckoning an account and transacting business, "May I obtain the seven riches of the superiors." When irrigating a field, "May I nurture the crop of mind-for-enlightenment." When planting, "May I plant the seed of mind-for-enlightenment in all beings." When yoking two bulls, "May I unite both wisdom and method." When plowing, "May I break up the solidity of the afflictions." When weeding, "May I weed out the afflictions." When reaping, "May I gather the crops of gnosis." When threshing, "May I remove the obscurations with their propensities." When washing grain, "May I obtain the fruit of perfect buddhahood." When climbing stairs, "May I climb to the top of the ten stages." When arriving at a house, "May I arrive at the stage of perfect buddhahood."

Learn to perform all actions in this way. The above was taught because it is easy to practice, but you should refer to *The Purification of the Environment Sutra* for a more explicit explanation. Such practice is called the "bodhisattva's attention to mental action."

Correct Accomplishment of Effort

Concerning correct accomplishment, *Entering the Bodhisattva's Practice* states:

Either directly or indirectly
Do not stray from beings' welfare.
Dedicate everything for enlightenment
For the sake of others' welfare.

The disciples act mainly from self-interest and only indirectly for others. Bodhisattvas act chiefly for others' welfare and indirectly for their own. You should eliminate nonbeneficial actions by means of antidote, or transform them into beneficial actions by means of skill in method. Aryadeva said:

Through intent the bodhisattva
Makes beneficial
Both the positive and the negative.
How? Because mind is master.

For one who has great method,
The afflictions become factors of enlightenment,
And samsara naturally pacific.
Thus bodhisattvas are inconceivable.

For example, not wasting things is acting indirectly for others, giving things to them is working directly for their welfare. If you work directly for others' welfare you will be happy and well liked in this life and in future lives will achieve your own welfare indirectly, having the best things and perfecting your practice of transcendent giving. Again, for example, learning dharma in order to teach it to others is acting indirectly for their benefit, while explaining dharma in order to clear the darkness of their ignorance is working directly for their welfare. The indirect self-benefit in this life from helping others with dharma is happiness due to skill in all aspects of dharma, to being numbered among the skillful, to suppression of all hindrances and receiving the confidence of everyone. In future lives you will obtain wisdom free from delusion about all things and will perfect your practice of transcendent wisdom through skillful methods.

Correct accomplishment consists of achievement of the four good qualities and elimination of the seven attachments. The four good qualities are removal of antithetical laziness, unconditioned realization of egolessness, fulfillment of what is necessary to achieve others' welfare, and development of beings and involving them in the three vehicles through such effort. The seven attachments are attachment to complacent laziness, and so on [see section 4.2.3 on correct morality].

Finally, there are both temporary and final benefits from making effort. Temporary benefits in this life include accomplishing worldly affairs and dharma work, and the resulting acquisition of friends, pleasures, further benefits, and religious fellowship. You'll be comfortable in this life and will have no regrets at the time of death. You will encounter no obstruction by human and nonhuman forces, and you will set an example for everyone. All at once, future negative impulses will be removed, and your essential good qualities will increase more and more. Those who make effort in this way will quickly obtain accomplishments and by means of them achieve all the qualities of perfect buddhahood.

Final benefits are that when perfect buddhahood is attained you'll have all the buddha qualities, such as the [ten] strengths and the [four] fearlessnesses [see Chapter 8], and your work on behalf of all beings will proceed without obstruction.

Meditative Absorption

Meditative absorption is mental equanimity aimed at attaining perfect buddhahood. When developed along with preparation, actual realization states, and postrealization practice, it becomes transcendent absorption. To understand the nature of absorption, you must know its antithesis, the antidotes, and correct accomplishment.

The Antithesis of Meditative Absorption

Its antithesis is distractibility, the inability to concentrate or to focus your attention one-pointedly on a mental objective, or focusing on an incorrect objective like nonbuddhists, or focusing correctly but in a manner conducive only to nirvana or higher rebirth [not to enlightenment].

The fault of this in the present life is that a person with a distractible mind cannot enter the dharma stream [leading to liberation]. He brings misery on himself inevitably, like an inexperienced rider mounting a wild stallion, and this misery induces all kinds of wrong behavior. At the time of death, he'll regret having led a useless life but will die anyway. It also destroys happiness in future lives. Like a waterfall plunging over a steep cliff or obsession with wealth, a distractable mind is difficult to control, and by causing nonbeneficial behavior binds one to samsara and leads to lower rebirth. Even attainment of mental equanimity can be wrong, as in nonbuddhist practices, as stated in *The King of Concentration Sutra*:

> When a worldly person meditates on voidness
> He's unable to correct belief in existence
> Because he's subject to emotional afflictions.

Further, incorrect voidness meditation, even when combined with love and compassion, will not lead to liberation from samsara; at best, it merely leads to higher rebirth. Even correct voidness meditation, if not directed by skillful method, leads only to the disciples' cessation [nirvana], not actual buddhahood.

The Antidotes to Distraction

The cause of distractibility is attachment to beings and enjoyments, and its antidotes are elimination of attachment and realizing the advantages of solitude. Eliminate attachment to beings by reflecting on statements like these from *Entering the Bodhisattva's Practice*:

When attached to beings,
Reality is totally obscured,
The attitude of renunciation destroyed,
And painful sorrow inevitably ensues.

A friend one moment
Becomes an enemy the next,
Irritated even in good times,
It's hard to please ordinary people.

They despise the poor
And criticize the rich—
How can you find happiness
With such ill-natured people?

Nothing pleases the immature
Save their own interests,
Thus the Tathagata said:
Never associate with such "children."

Jealous of superiors, competitive toward equals,
Proud toward inferiors, arrogant when praised,
Angered even at pleasant speech;
Of what use are such children?

Those who rely on others
Destroy themselves thereby,
Neglecting their own affairs
They won't achieve even their own goals,
So flee far from these "children."

> Like a bee gathering honey from flowers,
> Extract the pure meaning of Dharma,
> Then abide without companions,
> As though everyone's a stranger.

Eliminate attachment to enjoyments also. Obsession with enjoyments is always detrimental. In the beginning, while accumulating wealth, you don't see its negative aspects: the strife it creates with friends, competitors, and people you don't even know! Wealth acquired in a manner not harmonious with dharma is detrimental from the very beginning. Next, when hoarding your wealth, you'll be tormented day and night by fear of losing it, a slave to your attachment. Your work will be unceasing, constantly protecting your wealth and losing friends because of this. It will ruin your happiness in this life, and what can it do for you in the next, save being the cause of lower rebirth? Finally, it will exhaust the merit gained in past lives, resulting in problems like false friends, greedy relatives, strong enemies, and eventual loss of wealth. The faults of attachment to possessions were discussed in the section on giving [4.1.1].

About the advantages of solitude, Śāntideva says in *Entering the Bodhisattva's Practice*:

> In caves, in sacred and desolate places,
> And at the base of trees abiding,
> Not once looking back,
> I'll free myself of attachment.

> Using simple things: begging bowl,
> Clothes undesirable even to robbers,
> Or just leaving my body naked,
> I'll live always free of worries.

> No friends, no enemies
> This single body living alone;
> Planning thus an early "death"
> There'll be no sorrow when I die.

> So, relaxed and happy
> In productive surroundings,

All distractions gone,
In solitude I'll practice constantly.

Moreover, all pleasures quickly vanish, like the beauty of a water lily, because they are impermanent. Realize that this is so, reflect on scriptural statements concerning the causes of unhappiness, and go live in solitude.

The antidote of the mental distractibility resulting from these causes is meditative absorption, of which there are three types: those common to most meditative systems, those of the disciples' system, and those unique to the great vehicle. The first type consists of the preparatory practices and actual states of the first [through eighth] absorption levels. The instructions for this are given in the section on the mundane meditation path [6.4.1]. The preparatory practices and actual meditative states of the disciples' system are begun after reflecting on the faults of samsara, such as impermanence. Since their system differs from the great vehicle in aim, sequence, etc., I won't discuss them here. **4.5.A**

I will discuss only the practices of the great vehicle. The system of the Mind Only school is based on the works of Asanga and his brother Vasubandhu and can be learned from texts like *The Digest of the Great Vehicle* and *The Stages of a Bodhisattva's Practice*, so I won't discuss it here. I will explain the system of the Middle Way school as presented in the chapter on absorption in *Entering the Bodhisattva's Practice*, which is based on the intention of Nāgārjuna and his disciple Āryadeva. This system is also presented in Nāgārjuna's *Meditation on the Intent for Enlightenment*.

It will be easier to produce the intent for enlightenment if you first meditate the four infinitudes, so I'll explain them here. Infinite love is the merciful desire that beings find happiness. Infinite compassion is the desire that they be freed from misery. Infinite joy is the desire that they not lose such happiness and freedom. Infinite neutrality is the desire to neutralize the eight worldly concerns.[15] The infinititudes of love and compassion should be practiced as an integrated process.

---

[15] The eight worldly concerns are usually given as gain and loss, fame and disgrace, praise and blame, and pleasure and pain.

Meditation on Love.   In the meditation on love, the objects are beings who haven't entered the dharma stream of bliss and mental neutrality toward both happiness and misery, and also those who've entered the stream but haven't yet obtained the spiritual qualities of a bodhisattva or buddha.

The system of meditation[16] is explained in several sutras as the meditation on all beings as our mothers, because it's easy to cultivate love when you realize the interrelatedness of all beings. Some tantras, such as *Vajra Tip*, explain it as meditation on all beings as our children, and essentially, since every living being has been our father or other close relative in some lifetime, you should consider all beings close and dear. Further, it's not enough to provide mere temporary happiness; meditate from the marrow of your bones, "May all beings have happiness *and the source of happiness*." "Happiness" means physical and mental comfort in harmony with spirituality, and the "source of happiness" means their own involvement in spiritual practice which leads to final happiness. Practice this repeatedly until you develop a love for all beings like a mother for her only son.

The temporal benefits of this meditation are rebirth in higher realms and advantages such as being loved in return. The final benefit is buddhahood.

Rich food of a hundred flavors
Offered punctually every day
Has no comparison in its merit
To just one single instant of love. (PG)

Meditation on Compassion.   The objects of the meditation on compassion are the ten types of beings listed in *The Crown of Great Vehicle Sutras*:

Completely aflame, overpowered by enemies,
Oppressed by misery, obscured by darkness,

---

[16]The seven-step method for generating the intent for enlightenment by meditation on all beings as our mother includes the generation of love and compassion as its fourth and fifth steps. The full practice is given in *The Door of Liberation*, Chapter 5, "The Three Principles of the Path."

Entangled in a frustrating path,
Tightly bound with strong shackles,
Addicted to mixing good food with poison,
Lost on the path,
Traveling the wrong path with weakness—
Have compassion for such beings.

Such beings are completely aflame with attachment to sensual pleasures and happiness, overpowered by enemies and diverted from virtuous behavior by the [four] devils,[17] totally oppressed by the miseries of the three lower existences, obscured by the darkness of improper behavior like killing through ignorance of the results of such actions, entangled in a frustrating path within the confines of samsara, bound with the strong shackles of nonbuddhist beliefs, mixing the good food of Dharma with the poison of nonproductive addiction to the bliss of the absorption states that ruins their chance for the true bliss of enlightenment, lost on the path because of pretentious pride that leads them away from the path to liberation, traveling the wrong path of the nondefinitive lesser vehicle, and having weakness which makes them unable to complete the two accumulations [of merit and wisdom.] Are you like that?

The antitheses of the six transcendences are also objects of compassion:

Mercy for the stingy, mercy for the ill-behaved,
Mercy for the agitated, mercy for the careless,
Compassion for those distracted by objects,
Compassion for those with wrong beliefs. (CS)

Nirvana and samsara alike are objects of compassion. The disciples and solitary buddhas achieve neither their own nor others' welfare [by attaining nirvana]. Even ordinary individuals

---

[17]The "four devils" represent samsaric hindrance to liberation; they represent one's mundane psychophysical constituents (aggregrates), negative mental states, death, and external obstructions.

will attain buddhahood, but those two will be delayed forty eons. The causes and resultant miseries of samsara are objects of compassion. The former includes those impelled to improper behavior by bad companions and obsession with pleasures, and those who harm the Three Jewels and holy persons or are involved in dharma in an improper manner. These last are special objects of compassion because they are shot like arrows into lower rebirths. "Resultant miseries" includes those who are hungry, poor, sick, aged, discouraged, overcome with grief, who are separated from friends, in the hands of enemies, who have fallen from better circumstances, or who can't get what they need.

There are four causal factors in the development of compassion:

> A bodhisattva's compassion arises
> From happiness and misery and their basis.
> A bodhisattva's compassion arises
> From cause, teacher, and its own nature. (CS)

The first couplet indicates the objective causal factor, [the threefold misery] of the change inherent in happiness, the outright misery of misery and the misery of compounded things, which underlies the first two. The second couplet indicates the direct cause, the innate impulse for compassion, the controlling causal factor [*causa efficiens*], the spiritual teacher, and the ongoing causal factor, the developing attitude of compassion itself.

There are three basic types of compassion. Nonbuddhists meditate a compassion directed toward persons, aspiring to free what they believe to be existent, unitary, independent beings from existent, unitary, independent miseries. The disciples meditate a compassion directed toward things, aspiring to free beings, who are merely the temporary association of the five psychophysical aggregates, eighteen elements and twelve media from miseries that they view as existent phenomena. Followers of the great vehicle don't meditate in these ways, because such concepts are contradictory to the wisdom of the voidness [of persons and things]. Bodhisattvas meditate great compassion that is without objective,

thinking: "I will free these illusory beings from the misery and its causes, which are also illusory." [See Chapter 3 for further details.]
4.5.B
The importance of compassion is summed up by Avalokitesvara in *The Sutra Epitomizing All Dharma*:

> Bhagavan, a bodhisattva need not learn a lot of Dharma. A bodhisattva understands one thing well and by grasping that has all buddhadharma in the palm of his hand. Which one is that? It is great compassion.

Producing the Intent for Enlightenment.   When familiarized with the meditations of love and compassion, you may easily produce the intent for enlightenment through the three practices of equivalence of self and others, exchange of self and others, and finalization.

Meditation on the Equivalence of Self and Others.

> Meditate diligently from the start
> The equivalence of the happiness and misery
> Of yourself and others,
> And thus protect everyone as you would yourself. (EBP)

First practice equivalence meditation as follows. All life-forms in the universe have been linked to us in some way in former lives. Ascertain this interrelatedness of all life through scripture and logic. Reflect on it until a pleasurable state of tolerance arises, and then meditate from the depths of your heart, "May all beings have happiness and the causes of happiness like mine." If you experience some misery, meditate from the very marrow of your bones, "May I and all beings be free from such misery and its causes."
If you fail to produce the proper intent because of an attitude like that of the disciples, who feel, "I don't expect others to remove my misery, why should I remove theirs?" consider the following. The "self" is impermanent; why strive to

gather food and clothing for the future when in the very next instant your "self" is gone and replaced by a different "self"? It's erroneous and illogical to think that this "self" will exist tomorrow, and furthermore, "It's incorrect to think, 'This is experienced by me'" [from EBP].

For example, ordinary people think, "Last year this river carried away my clothes," or "Tomorrow I will cross this stream." But it's not the very same water that carried away the clothes or that will be crossed tomorrow. Likewise, neither past mind nor future mind is your "self"; they are different things. The future mind, is, however, included in your mental continuum [samtāna], so it *does* make sense to work for your own liberation. Likewise, you should work for others' welfare, with the understanding that although they are not a part of you, they are inextricably connected with you. You might feel that it's impossible to achieve both your own and others' welfare, that you must work only for yourself. But it says in Entering the Bodhisattva's Practice, "A pain in the foot is not in the hand," meaning that although the hand is not pained by a thorn in the foot, the hand will still remove the thorn from the foot, or a cinder from the eye, or put food into the mouth. Similarly, parents act for the well-being of their children. The idea that you must work exclusively for self-welfare is very wrong, for in fact, it's almost impossible to achieve your own welfare without working for that of others also.

The Method of Exchanging Self and Others.   The method of exchanging self and others is essentially the offering of your happiness to others and willingness to take on their misery. The visualization technique [for removing the compulsive nature of negative emotions and attitudes by utilizing those very emotions and attitudes] is summarized in Entering the Bodhisattva's Practice:

> Take lower, equal, and higher as self
> And self as that very other;
> Then with mind free of preconceptions
> Meditate jealousy, competitiveness, and pride.

To practice by utilizing jealousy, visualize a situation where a person in an inferior position felt anger toward you in a superior position. Then [exchange positions with that person and] meditate on the jealousy that person had toward you. When this visualization takes effect, you'll actually experience such jealousy. Think, "If such misery as this occurs, it is not right to evoke jealousy in others." In this way your own tendencies for jealousy will be reduced.

To practice by utilizing competitiveness, visualize a situation where there was an all-out conflict between yourself and a person of equal strength. Then [exchange positions] and meditate on your aggressiveness toward that person. When the visualization takes effect, you'll experience your aggressiveness as felt by that person. Consider the harm done to that person, thinking, "If such misery occurs, it is not right to be competitive toward others." Thus your own aggressive tendencies will be reduced.

To practice by utilizing pride, exchange positions with someone inferior to yourself and meditate pride about such things as status, talents, or wealth, from that person in the superior position toward yourself as inferior. When you can feel the effects of that pride toward yourself, think, "If such misery occurs, it isn't right for me to have pride toward others." Thus your prideful tendencies will be reduced *by the essence of pride itself*. The subtler aspects of this practice are described in *Entering the Bodhisattva's Practice*.

If you want a less complicated method, recite these prayers and meditate on their meaning:

> May their sins ripen to me
> And all my virtues accrue to them.
> As long as just one being
> Remains unliberated anywhere,
> Even if I've attained perfect enlightenment
> I will take his place. (PG)

> May all the pain of living beings,
> Whatsoever, come to me,
> And with my bodhisattva's virtues
> May I provide happiness for them. (EBP)

You might think it would be unbearable to take on the misery of all beings, but this is a misconception. Just as calling wild birds and animals won't make them come, *wishing* to take on the misery of others won't make it actually happen. Instead, the misery of yourself and others will be extinguished. Some people claim that the exchange of self and others is not a good method for producing the intent for enlightenment because such extreme concern about others' misery will be unbearable. Their mistake is that they don't understand the difference between extreme concern toward specific objectives and correct nonextreme concern as a purely subjective experience. When you understand this key to the exchange of self and others, you'll quickly produce the intent for enlightenment.

Finalization Practice.   The finalization practice involves recalling the faults of self-interest and the benefits of working for others by thoroughly understanding why it is necessary to work for others: [All your misery comes from self-interest, others' misery is no different than yours, and your own goal is best achieved by working for others.] All your own misery comes from self-interest:

> Although that is the precept,
> If you, mind, don't observe it,
> It's right for me to destroy you.
> Previously you destroyed me
> As if I were your enemy;
> Knowing this now, wherever you are,
> I'll completely crush your arrogance
> And destroy the mind
> Which cares for itself.

> I've sold you to others—
> Don't be sad, be grateful.
> If I didn't prudently
> Give you to beings,
> You'd surely have given me
> To the guardians of hell.

You did so many times,
And I suffered long from those betrayals.
Now, recalling it in anger,
I'll destroy your self-centered attitude.

As if under a spell
I am trapped here unaware
That the source of deception
Dwells within myself.

If the jailers of samsara's prison
And the executioners of hell
Dwell in my heart, in the cage
Of attachments, I will never be happy.

When I vowed to free from affliction
All living beings in the ten directions
To the ends of the universe,
I was not yet freed from affliction myself!

Speaking thus, not realizing my own
Measure, was I not mad?
Thus I must never give up
Fighting the afflictions.

I'll aim for this:
I'll fight with a vengeance
All kinds of afflictions, save only
The affliction of fighting affliction. (EBP)

Beware that the meditations of equivalence and exchange may not produce immediate result, and also, if not handled firmly, your mind may react like a wild horse struck by a whip. If this happens, impress on your mind the pain of others, and when you can vividly visualize their suffering, forcibly eliminate selfishness and offer whatever help those beings need.

With such consideration for others
Provide them with help;

Be prepared to give
Even things vital to your own life. (EBP)

Since your pain is no different than others', meditate jealousy from yourself to yourself, considering your own happy, superior state and their miserable inferior condition:

I am happy, others are miserable.
I am superior, others inferior.
I have help, others do not—
Why not be jealous of myself?

I'll give up my happiness
And take on others' misery
Whatever happiness I have
I now offer to all beings.

I'll examine my own faults:
"I did such a thing at such a time,"
And even take responsibility
For the faults of others. (EBP)

Examine your physical, verbal, and mental behavior. If you've behaved badly, shame yourself, thinking: "You are wandering in samsara because of past behavior like this. Now, still not aware, you are straying further into samsara and lower rebirths." When other people harm you, don't feel it's solely their fault but is also the result of your own bad actions. Don't try to hide even the smallest faults in behavior from others. You can avoid feeling proud when praised by emphasizing the other person's good qualities and thinking, "These good qualities of mine are just minor and ephemeral; I'm really full of faults." But *care must be taken at this stage of practice*:

Like stretching the neck,
Don't do it too hard,
Or like the decorum of a bride,
Practice such shame with care and caution.

Finally, eliminate self-centeredness because working for others is the best way to achieve your own goal. This was taught by the perfect Buddha, who always spoke the truth. You'll see the advantages of this later on.

Some practictioners wonder whether meditation on voidness should be begun only after the intent for enlightenment has been produced. *Voidness meditation should not be practiced while cultivating the intent for enlightenment* by exchange of self and others, because it is dangerous to meditate voidness without cutting through conceptualization by means of wisdom [and conceptualization is necessary during the practice of exchange]. Nāgārjuna warned, "Drawing near the experience of voidness, those of small wisdom will be destroyed."

The Correct Accomplishment of Meditative Absorption

Correct accomplishment consists of attainment of the four spiritual qualities and the elimination of seven attachments. The four qualities are freedom from mental distractibility; unconditioned realization of egolessness; attainment of skill in meditative absorption, which is prerequisite to accomplishing the welfare of yourself and others; and ability to further the mental development of beings by involving them in practice. The seven attachments are attachment to mental distraction, procrastination, complacency, expectation of return, expectation of results, attraction to the latent tendencies of mental distractibility, and misdirection which is of two types: attraction to the lesser vehicle and to concepts.

The temporal benefits of cultivating the absorptions in the present life include attainment of tranquilization and the resultant suppression of ephemeral afflictions, neutralization of the eight worldly concerns, experience of the bliss and joy of the absorption states, and attainment of supernormal abilities and superknowledges.[18] The temporal benefits in future lives include physical,

---

[18]See section 8.6.

verbal, and mental fitness, the four absorptions of the material realm and the five superknowledges. The ultimate benefits are that in the state of buddhahood you will have such qualities as the fourfold ability in working for others, as indicated in *The Crown of Great Vehicle Sutras*:

> Taking birth, living in and leaving [existences],
> Emanations, transformations,
> Concentration and gnosis.

Wisdom

Wisdom is realizing that the basic nature of phenomena is voidness. When established through preparation, actual realization states, and postrealization practice, it becomes transcendent wisdom. The nature of wisdom is explained in terms of its antitheses, their antidotes, and correct development.

The Antithesis of Wisdom

Its antitheses are corrupt forms of wisdom: failure to seek the benefits of wisdom like fools, seeking it incorrectly like nonbuddhists, or seeking it correctly but not using it to attain perfect enlightenment, like the disciples. There are many faults of this in the present life: lack of skill, not knowing what should and should not be done, being despised by everyone, and unworthiness to be considered truly experienced. Canakya said in his *Maxims*: "Without the treasure of learning, one is blind." In future lives:

> Without fine discernment of phenomena
> There's no way to still the afflictions;
> Those without it flounder in samsara's ocean. (TA)

Without wisdom you won't know what actions are beneficial or detrimental, and thus all your activities will be ineffectual. Wherever you are reborn, you'll have weak faculties and won't be able to find even one word of dharma. In meditation you'll be unable to cut the root of egoism, or even if you do, you'll fall into cessation of personal existence through lack of skill in methods, like the disciples and solitary buddhas.

Corrupt Wisdom

The basic cause of corrupt wisdom is ignorance and the subsidiary condition is reliance on false teachers.

> Ignorance is the root of evil
> And of belief in a personal ego;
> In addition, a bad teacher
> Smothers you in darkness. (EVC)

The antidotes are learning and reflecting on methods for removing these causes. Learning reduces the propensity for ignorance, but you must learn from a real, virtuous spiritual friend who teaches the three divisions of canonical scriptures and four classes of tantra in a noncontradictory manner.

Don't accept a teacher who expounds some made-up teaching that conflicts with what you know to be correct dharma. Even though they may appear good in their activities, they are like butchers selling donkey meat as real beef.

The Antidotes to Corrupt Wisdom

The antidotes for corrupt wisdom resulting from these causes will be treated in two sections: rejection of wrong views and achievement of correct wisdom.

Rejection of Wrong Views

The views of the various nonbuddhist systems are either materialistic or nihilistic and the great spiritual masters of Tibet have examined them and found them to be wrong. They were created by people under the influence of egoism and promulgated by false spiritual teachers with either materialistic or nihilistic attitudes. **4.6.A** Such wrong views are corrected by freeing the mind of the extremisms of materialism or nihilism through realizing the absence of an inherent identity in anything: the nonexistence of personal ego and of identities of things.

Wrong views of buddhist sects are of three types. The first are the tenets of the disciples of the Differentiators school [Vaibhāṣika] and Sutra Followers school [Sautrāntika]. **4.6.B** The second type involves the mistaken idea that the implicit teachings of the great vehicle have explicit [literal] meaning, which can be found in the True Aspect and False Aspect subsystems of the Mind Only school, and in the Self-Proven and Dialectical sub-systems of the Middle Way school. Although all buddhist schools claim to uphold the "middle way," if the tenets of *any* system fail to avoid the extremes of materialism and nihilism, they should be rejected. Detailed analyses of their tenets may be found in my *Treasury of Logic* and *Classification of Tenets*.[19]

The third type of wrong view includes systems based on the belief that there are teachings of Buddha not contained in the canonical scriptures of the lesser and great vehicles. One example is the teaching of the Chinese monk named "Meditation Master" Huashang Mahayana, who visited Tibet during the reign of Khri-srong lde'u-btsan and propagated a system called "Mere Blankness Is Sufficient." He taught that "since buddhahood is not attained by any dharma expressed by inherently essenceless words, mere blankness is sufficient" [meaning that direct realization of mind through meditation without thought or conceptualization is the way to attain buddhahood].[20]

---

[19] A translation of two texts of tenets of the four philosophical systems of buddhism was published in Herbert Guenther, *Buddhist Philosophy in Theory and Practice*, Berkeley: Shambala, 1971.

[20] His title "Meditation Master" (*dhyāna*) is the equivalent of the Chinese *Chan* and the Japanese *Zen*, which caused subsequent misunderstanding in Tibet that he was a teacher of Zen Buddhism, a view that has persisted into modern times. Although he did expound a "sudden" approach, as opposed to the "gradual" path of the Indian great vehicle systems, it is unlikely that he

[An excerpt from the famous "Lhasa debate of 792" between this Chinese monk and the Indian master Kamalaśīla is given in Part Two]. **4.6.C** Wise spiritual teachers said that this Chinese monk didn't know anything about real dharma, but even now true dharma is being neglected because of movements similar to the Mere Blankness system, believing that buddhahood is attained merely by realizing the "naked face of the mind." For example, some present-day teachers are giving these precepts for *mahāmudrā* practices:

The three strayings and four addictions—
Eliminate them and meditate the innate.
Like spinning a brahmanical thread,
It must be done evenly, steadily, without modification.

They explain the "three strayings of *mahāmudrā*" as becoming entrapped in mental ecstasy, clarity, and cessation of thought, and the "four addictions" as addiction to the state, the meditation, the path, and the intensifying of *mahāmudrā* experience: "Like spinning a [ritual] brahmanical thread, it should be done evenly, steadily, without modification easily and relaxed." This is very similar to the Mere Blankness system and is not the *mahāmudrā* taught in any of Buddha's scriptures, and in particular, the *mahāmudrā* explained in the tantras' *samayamudrā*. Nāgārjuna said, "Those who don't know *karmamudrā* [the union of male and female principles] won't realize *dharmamudrā*; how could they understand even the name of *mahāmudrā*?"

Several other systems focusing on the "clarity of the natural mind" have also been shown to be ignorant meditations and, as stated in *Attainment of Gnosis*, "By ignorance [only] ignorance is obtained." Of any "addiction," addiction to ignorant meditation is the worst. Addiction to meditative absorption will obstruct development of skillful method, progress on the path, and all

---

represented mainstream Chinese Zen. The debate was conducted in writing and the transcript was translated by Paul Demieville as *Le Concile de Lhasa* (Paris: 1952).

common and unique spiritual qualities. If you fail to focus your mind correctly on voidness, the basic condition of phenomena, attainment of buddhahood will be delayed as long as by moral offenses. Even the example of spinning Brahmanical thread just cited is incorrect. The wool must first be carded and then, when spun, must be tightened if too loose and loosened if too tight. If lumps and tangles are not corrected, you won't have good thread. Therefore, without "modification," you won't have anything but clumps of raw wool. Indeed, just picking up the raw wool is an act of modification. Likewise with *mahāmudrā*, if you can realize it without any modification of mind, what need is there for a teacher's instructions? What could be a greater modification than that very meditation on the innate which involves stopping the three strayings and four addictions?

A number of systems propose "mahāmudrā" practices that are actually the practice of transcendent wisdom.[21] Some rely on the statement in *The One Hundred Thousand Verse Transcendent Wisdom Sutra*, "All things have a nature like space," to infer the "three recognitions of *mahāmudrā*: recognition of all things as mind, of mind as space, and space as voidness." Others teach a *mahāmudrā* meditation without memory, awareness of attentional focusing by relying on the statement, "Absence of memory and attention is recollection of Buddha," and others practice *mahāmudrā* from the statement, "Anything mental is nonexistent, because mind is naturally clear light." I've seen many such oddities. If you don't know the correct way of meditating *mahāmudrā*, it will just be equivalent to transcendent wisdom meditation, which is practiced by developing your accumulation of knowledge into the wisdom derived from learning while living morally, and then reflecting logically on the correct meaning of what was learned to develop wisdom derived from reflection. After that, meditate on the correct meaning as it appears in the transcendence literature, producing the preparatory, actual realization and postrealization states [see the next section]. But this is not the *mahāmudrā* of the secret teachings.

---

[21]See Gampopa's *Jewel Ornament of Liberation*, p. 149.

Achievement of Wisdom

To reach the goal of perfect buddhahood, you must combine three things: the bow of compassion, the arrow of wisdom, and the expert archer of skillful method. About compassion, it says in *Entering the Middle Way*:

Buddhas are born from bodhisattvas.
Compassion and the intent for enlightenment
Are the source of bodhisattvas.

About wisdom as the arrow, from *In Praise of Superiority*:

Maheśvara with one wrathful arrow
Was said to have burnt three cities.
But you, with the one arrow of wisdom,
Burnt the afflictions *and* their latent propensities.

And from *Exposition of Valid Cognition*:

One is liberated by seeing voidness;
This is the goal of all other meditations.

Now just as it is necessary to join bow and arrow in order to hit the target, compassion and voidness must be united. Saraha said:

Even by voidness, when de-void of compassion,
The superior path will not be found;
And if compassion alone is practiced
You'll remain unliberated in samsara.

Voidness and compassion appear to be contradictory; skillful method is needed to integrate them in practice. By practicing compassion and wisdom integrated by skillful method you will quickly complete the accumulations of merit and wisdom, and without these you can't realize true voidness, mind's actual nature, and attain buddhahood. By knowing the superficial reality, you are skilled in all knowables, and through this others' welfare is accomplished. If you are not skilled, your own welfare won't even be achieved, to say nothing of that of others. Without even knowing the "dharma" of mankind, what can be said of superior Dharma?

But some people think, "Since buddhahood is attained when the nature of mind is realized, one should practice with the view that buddhahood is not attained by any other means. Why are any other assets necessary?" It is indeed true that buddhahood is attained when the mind is realized, but mind can't be realized without first perfecting the assets of merit and wisdom. For example, you can say that you light the wick of a lamp, but without oil the wick will not burn. You can say a person is killed by an arrow, but a bow and archer are also necessary. Consider this passage from *The Sutra Requested by Sagaramati*:

> A bodhisattva possesses wisdom, but if he feels that transcendent wisdom is the most superior and the other transcendences inferior, he will neglect meritorious activities and skillful method, and fail to practice giving, morality, patience, effort, and meditative absorption. Such excessive attachment to the experience of cessation of mental elaboration and thought is the iron hook of the devil of wisdom.

Such persons don't strive for merit and are unconcerned about evil due to the impact of their experience of the voidness, as Nāgārjuna said:

> Persons with little wisdom are destroyed
> By their faulty view of voidness,
> Like mishandling a poisonous snake
> Or the inept use of sorcery.
> The conquerors' voidness, it is said,
> Transcends all ideas.
> Those with ideas of voidness
> Have no accomplishment.

Or as stated in *The Sutra Requested by Kāśyapa*, "The mere Mount Everest of a belief in personal existence is easy [to remove], but the ideas of voidness of those full of prideful preconceptions are immovable." **4.6.D**

I'll explain this a bit more. Generally speaking, realization of mind must be either realization of mind-in-itself or realization of the mind's perception of an external object. Realization of merely mind-in-itself is a nonbuddhist idea and is wrong because it doesn't eliminate subject-object duality. Realization of the mind's perception of an external object is held by some nonbuddhist systems that consider objects to be creations of Mahesvara, natural matter [*prakṛti*], and the like, and by buddhist systems in which the objects are atoms for the disciples, mind for the Mind Only school, and dependently occurring things for the Middle Way school. You should examine any system of belief in the light of scripture and logic, and reject any that accept either existence or nonexistence, since they fail to avoid the extremes of materialistic or nihilistic views. The correct view of mind and apparent phenomena as dependent occurrences should be learned through scripture and logic; otherwise you cannot correctly realize personal egolessness and phenomenal identitylessness. If you don't realize personal egolessness, your practice will be no different from that of the nonbuddhists, and if phenomenal identitylessness isn't realized it will be no different than the disciples' meditation. It's necessary from the very beginning to remove preconceptions about egolessness and identitylessness by means of the wisdoms derived from learning and reflection, because correct realization depends on these two wisdoms. Without realization of egolessness and identitylessness, you won't achieve the wisdom derived from meditation and the experience of voidness of the insight path. Belief in existence won't be destroyed and any voidness meditation will only lead you back to samsara and lower rebirth. As stated in *The Exposition of Valid Cognition*, "Since the net of thought is ripped apart/One perceives with inherent clarity." **4.6.E**

Meditation on Voidness.   There are many systems for meditating on the basic condition, voidness. The disciples meditate on the four noble truths; the False Aspect division of the Mind Only school uses the fourfold yoga of Śāntipa: "one-pointed, of one taste, free from mental elaboration, and unmeditated"; the Self-

Proven Middle Way school meditates on the extreme unconditioned unification [of appearances and voidness]; and the Dialectical Middle Way system meditates on the extreme unconditioned voidness. The old secret teachings [of the Nyingma] employ the ultimate yoga [*atiyoga*], the highest of their nine vehicles, whereas the new secret teachings employ the four initiations and the gnoses of the two phases [of generation and completion]. The various tantric systems all have the same goal but differ in the sequence of objectives in meditation. Master Saroruha called it "unmistaken thatness"; the great yogin Virlapa said, "extreme pure thatness"; and Nāgārjuna said in *The Five Stages*, "ultimate unification of the five stages" and also "the four mudras of the two phases: *karmamudrā*, *dharmamudrā*, *samayamudrā*, and *mahāmudrā*." These diverse statements have but one intention, and they all involve the special practices of the four initiations and the two tantric phases. Since the profound key to this will be given when you receive the secret teachings, I won't discuss it here. Regarding *mahāmudrā*, to be real it must evolve from the practices of the secret teachings. People might think they are practicing *mahāmudrā*, but if it hasn't evolved from the gnoses of the two phases it isn't the actual *mahāmudrā* by which you can attain buddhahood in this very life. I've explained this so that you will be able to distinguish the different meditation systems and not mistake other meditations for the real *mahāmudrā* of the secret teachings, but you should learn these matters in depth directly from an experienced teacher.

Achievement of Correct Wisdom

Achievement of correct wisdom has three topics: preparatory stoppage of mental elaboration by correct view, actual realization of voidness—the goal of meditation practice—and postrealization follow-up practice, which finalizes that realization experience.

Preparatory Practice.   Preparatory practice consists of maintaining basic moral practice and stopping mental elaboration by means of correct views gained from training the mind through learning. You should learn from a teacher who knows the correct meaning of the transcendent wisdom literature, the logic of the Middle Way texts, and the key to distinguishing correct and incorrect dharma. If you don't have such a teacher, you should try to stop mental elaboration through correct view gained by studying works like *The Epitome of Precepts* and *Entering the Bodhisattva's Practice*. Without extensive learning, you won't understand the two realities, nor realize the deeper meaning of the scriptures. **4.6.F** Nāgārjuna said:

> The dharma teachings of the buddhas
> Are truly based on the two realities:
> Mundane superficial reality
> And absolute reality.
> Those who don't know the difference
> Between these two facets of reality
> Won't realize the profound thatness
> Which Buddha taught. (RVMW)

Concerning the two realities, Śāntideva said, "The absolute is not a cognizable object; 'cognition' implies the superficial." Some people take this as a definition of superficial reality as cognizable objects and absolute reality as that which transcends cognizable objects, ["cognizable" understood as implying cognition of ordinary persons]. But this is not the most accurate way of defining them. I would define the superficial as that which is perceived as an existent thing in a nonanalytic cognition, and the absolute as that which is not perceived as an existent thing in an analytic cognition. The term "reality" denotes a valid [noncontradictory] cognition. **4.6.G** All apparent phenomena are superficial. That which is not perceived as a truly existing thing [in an analytic cognition] is absolute. There are true and false superficials. True superficials are apparent things perceived by valid cognition, the manifold appearances resulting from the common consensus of beings, which are capable of meaningful function, but which upon analysis cannot be found to be truly existent. False superficials are appearances in nonvalid cognition; [they are not "reality" but are] mistaken perceptions incapable of meaningful function, like visual aberrations, double vision, mirage, and the like.

Considered from the viewpoint of persons:

People without insight accept
A samsara and a nirvana.
Those with insight don't accept
Duality of samsara and nirvana. **4.6.H** (TWS)

The Dialectical Middle Way school holds that "cognitions of ordinary persons are superficial, the realization states of persons experiencing voidness are absolute, their postrealization states are superficial, and nirvana is exclusively absolute." This is slightly incomplete, however, since it doesn't include gnosis [which is the simultaneous perception of the apparent and absolute]. I feel it's better to say that the superficial is the apparent aspect of things, the absolute is their void aspect, and their nondual aspect is unification, as taught in the secret teachings.

When, after realizing appearances
And voidness separately,
The two are truly integrated
This is explained as unification. (FS)

Thus the goal is perception of things as-they-are through meditation practice directed toward unification of method and wisdom, by which one gradually progresses though the ten bodhisattva stages and five paths, obtaining buddhahood as the final result. This is the intention of all scriptures of explicit meaning.

Regarding the question of whether the two realities are the same or different, they are not merely synonyms for the same things, since that stance incurs four faults, such as the absolute as being perceivable just like the superficial. The idea that they are completely different also incurs four faults, such as the lack of an absolute reality in the phenomenal. *The Untangling the Knot Sutra* states, "If they are the same, the absolute would be an existent, and if opposites, the absolute would be nonexistent." The absolute is neither existent nor nonexistent, as stated in *The One Hundred Thousand Verse Sutra*, "Its sole characteristic is the lack of characteristic," and in *The Epitome of Transcendent Wisdom*, "It lacks duality of existence and nonexistence." The definitive statement in *The Exposition of Valid Cognition* is:

> Since nonexistence is not itself a thing
> It can't be an object of analytic cognition,
> [But] these conventional terms are used
> To explain the [process of] analysis. **4.6.I-K**

Actual Realization State. Meaningful meditation practice begins after stopping mental elaboration by correct view. You should have previously taken the uncommon [bodhisattva] refuge vow and produced the intent for enlightenment. Sit on a comfortable cushion in an isolated place, with legs crossed, hands in meditation mudra [palms up and slightly cupped with left hand on top], spine straight and eyes lowered toward the tip of the nose, and meditate the transcendent wisdom concentration aimed at realizing personal egolessness and phenomenal identitylessness. After each session, dedicate the merit of meditation to attainment of perfect buddhahood for the sake of other beings. Devote one session each day to meditating compassion without specific objective, and also continue the work of learning and reflecting on the teachings concerning the dreamlike nature of all apparent phenomena. The actual keys to this practice should be learned directly from an experienced teacher. [See Chapter 6 for further discussion.]

Postrealization Practice. Realizational experiences must be finalized by follow-up practice, which includes that of ordinary individuals and that of superiors [who have experienced true insight into voidness]. The techniques for ordinary individuals vary according to the various levels of the accumulation and applications paths [see Chapter 6], but for simplicity I will condense them into the three topics of purification of behavior, development of wisdom, and perfecting of concentration, which are termed the "special practices of morality, wisdom, and concentration." This consists of perfecting wisdom on a foundation of pure moral behavior, because with such wisdom your concentration will not go astray.

This voidness meditation, king of concentrations,
Is borne on the head of pure morality.
Though constantly meditating on the nature of things
The immature, striving incorrectly, have no realization.
(KC)

"Striving incorrectly" indicates the ineffectual efforts of foolish immature persons who learn without maintaining moral behavior or try to meditate without first learning. There are three types of morality, which should be practiced in succession. First, purify the three doors [of physical, verbal, and mental action] with the morality of vows, like cleaning out a vessel. Then acquire beneficial mental assets through the morality of gathering virtues, like filling the vessel with nectar. Then work for the welfare of all beings with the morality for accomplishing others' welfare, like curing a sick person by administering the nectar. [See section 4.2.2.] Perform all activities in the light of transcendent wisdom, purifying the three concepts of agent, recipient, and object involved.

Sutras like *Good Practice* and *Maitreya's Supplication*, and texts like *The Precious Garland* and *Entering the Bodhisattva's Practice* state that the finalization of perfect buddhahood will be quickly achieved by performing the seven branches of worship. In addition, the ten practices for strengthening refuge and the intent for enlightenment should also be performed three times each day and night. This is especially relevant to developing skillful methods.

The finalization practice of superiors [on the insight path] is explained in Chapter 6, which treats the paths and stages.

Correct Accomplishment of Wisdom

Correct accomplishment consists of attaining four spiritual qualities and eliminating seven attachments. The four qualities are freedom from corrupt wisdom, unconditioned realization of personal egolessness and phenomenal identitylessness, helping others by removing their doubts through wisdom, and thus being able to further their development by involving them in the three vehicles. The seven attachments are: attachment to corrupt wisdom, complacency, expectation of return, expectation of results, attraction to the latent tendencies of corrupt wisdom, and to misdirection [attraction to the lesser vehicle and belief in the three concepts].

The temporal benefits of cultivating wisdom in the present life include many assets like skillful intellect, unshakable self-reliant knowledge about everything, the unleashing of your wisdom through effective communication and having its resultant satisfaction, skillfulness, and setting an example for the whole world. Temporal benefits in future lives include acute faculties, exceptional wisdom and the ability to retain learning wherever you are reborn, elimination of your blockage to omniscience, ability to recreate the glorious teachings of the buddhas and bodhisattvas and turn the wheel of Dharma correctly for others.

The ultimate benefits are that when buddhahood is attained you will perceive all things both as they appear and as they really are [simultaneously], you will have a self-reliant intellect through the four analytic knowledges, and you can overcome all antagonists with the fourfold fearlessness [see Chapter 8].

5

The Four Social Means

Having explained the six transcendences that are practiced to develop your own spiritual qualities, we'll now consider the four social means for aiding the development of other beings. They are: giving, effective communication, acting for others, and setting an example. Their common characteristic is helping beings in your environment by skillful methods aimed at their spiritual development.

Giving

First, attract people by offering gifts to create the opportunity to teach dharma. This is essentially the same as the practice of transcendent giving explained before [section 4.1]. You should avoid impure giving and cultivate pure giving.

Effective Communication

"Effective communication" means teaching dharma in order to develop the people you've attracted by giving. When doing this you should reject incorrect dharma, not contradict scripture or logic, not confuse explicit and implicit [i.e., literal and implied] meanings, not confuse hidden intentions, indirect intentions and direct intentions. Don't mix higher teachings intended for superior persons with the lower teachings for ordinary persons. You should explain topics common to both lesser and greater vehicles in a noncontradictory manner and clearly distinguish topics unique to each. You should explain that the practices of the transcendences and the secret teachings both have the same goal, and when dealing with persons practicing the secret teachings your explanations should agree with the four classes of tantra. In essence, you should teach with an understanding of the nature of those being taught, of the different classes of dharma and the various ways of explaining them. About the importance of teaching according to the nature of the student, Candrakīrti said:

A teacher knows the student's mind
And teaches accordingly.
The skillful should gather disciples,
The foolish should never.

And Śāntideva advised:

Don't teach the vast and profound to inferior persons.
Always afford equal respect
To lower and higher teachings.
Don't force lower teachings
On those fit to receive the Vast Dharma.
Don't neglect any practice.
Don't confuse sutra and tantra. (EBP)

Acting for Others

"Acting for others" means encouraging others to practice. If the people you've taught don't undertake serious practice, induce them to do so by skillful methods. For example, if someone has doubt about being able to produce the intent for enlightenment, you should say, "Don't worry, even [the bodhisattva] Mañjuśrī had deceitful, hypocritical attitudes and did many bad things, but was able to produce the intent for enlightenment and will eventually attain buddhahood. So why can't you also do it?"

Some people fail to produce the intent for enlightenment because they feel it won't be carried over to the next life. You should tell them, "Even if you are not aware of it, the intent won't really be lost, just as forgetting a bad deed won't prevent its results. Or as, when you associate with crude people, you put aside polite behavior, but you haven't really lost your manners." Asaṅga said, "If you produce the intent for enlightenment now, you'll never forget it no matter where you're reborn." And from *The Birth Stories*:

> The results of action are inconceivable;
> Even one with compassion can be reborn an animal,
> So don't lose your motivation for Dharma.

Get people started with easier practices. Some people feel unable to produce the intent because of statements in some scriptures emphasizing the difficulty of living up to it, such as "Don't hesitate to give your head, hand, or foot," or that it takes a long time, even eons. Tell them that according to many sutras, it's sufficient to give just a glass of water.

> Gifts of vegetables and such
> Are made as a start;
> Later, when accustomed to that,
> You'll be able to give your own flesh.

> But your body should not be sacrificed
> If you don't have the absolute intent;
> Why sacrifice the chance to accomplish
> The great purpose now and in the future? (EBP)

Explain that "beginners should give small things according to your ability. Later, after obtaining tolerance toward birthlessness, you'll make no distinction between a vegetable and your own body, and then be able to give your own flesh." Similarly, with regard to morality, tell them, "Just keep the vow of temporary abstinence or the four basic vows for a day, a month, or a year, according to your ability. Then when you can't even be forced to misbehave, you'll be able to keep [more stringent] vows. Start developing patience by practicing for just one day or toward one person, and then gradually extend it. Commence effort by practicing virtue for just one day, and then gradually extend it. First meditate for just one session, and eventually you'll attain the actual absorption states. Even with wisdom, by learning to extract the meaning of just a single verse you'll eventually correctly realize the import of all three baskets of scripture." Encourage them to practice by inspiring them in this way.

> When you're accustomed there will be
> Nothing that isn't easy;
> By becoming accustomed to small harm
> You'll be able to tolerate great harmships.

Setting an Example

"Setting an example" means involving yourself in virtuous activities in order to induce others to do the same. Although you've taught and gotten people started practicing, they might not make much effort out of laziness or lack of motivation. When this happens, involve yourself in particular practices to set an example. Suppose you've urged someone to make offerings to a teacher of the Three Jewels because "it has great merit," but that person says "I'm unable to give." Tell him, "I'm going to make an offering, will you assist me?" And he might reply, "Well, I suppose I'll help you," and thus becomes involved. If someone says, "I'm unable to practice the six transcendences, or even listen to dharma teachings," tell her, "I'm going to go hear some teachings." And she might reply, "Oh well, I'll go also."

A long time ago a bodhisattva named Beautiful Hair entered a city and saw a woman walking around with the body of her dead son tied to her back, unable to accept his death. So he took a similar body from the cemetery and followed her. The woman saw that this was unhealthy and, after talking it over, they both decided to give up the corpses.

> The work of leading everyone to bliss
> Cannot be bought at any price,
> So you should gladly rejoice
> In the spiritual qualities attained by others.

> To one who teaches well
> Utter, "Well said!"
> Seeing someone acting virtuously,
> Give him joy by offering praise.

> When beholding people,
> Look in a manner both open and humble
> Saying, "By helping each other
> Together, we'll attain buddhahood." (EBP)

The Relationship Between the Four Social Means and the Six Transcendences

You might think that the content of the four social means is included in the six transcendences. This is indeed so, but the transcendences are practiced mainly for your own development, whereas the social means are aimed at the development of other people. Giving provides temporary help to others, whereas the other three are sources of final help because they promulgate the teachings of the six transcendences, involve trainees in practice, and provide further inducement to practice. They are four in number because they attract people to Dharma, start them in practice, help them to practice, and help them finalize their practice. All methods for developing beings are included in these four.

6

The Five Paths

The lines of the root verse, "Entering the faultless" and "Purification of the environment," refer to the five paths and ten stages of a person practicing "superior Dharma" [that is, preparation for and experiential realization of voidness]. The term "path" denotes access to a liberative process. Some consider it the outcome of a process, but this is incorrect. It is like a gateway to the actual process; a person who has concluded a process is no longer involved in it. The five paths are the accumulation, application, insight, meditation, and final paths. I will explain them according to the great vehicle system.

Accumulation Path

The accumulation path provides access to the initial liberative process of general practice for suppressing mental conditionings [by the power of the dual accumulation of merit and gnosis]. It has three degrees of strength: the weak degree involves the meditations called "four foci of awareness" and is not certain to lead to the application path, the moderate degree involves practice of the "four real efforts" and is certain to lead to the application path eventually, the strong degree involves cultivation of the "four bases of super-normal powers" and leads into the first phase of the application path in the present life.[22]

Concerning level or mode of mental functioning, the basic moral practice [for accumulating merit] is supported by the mental level of the desire realm, and the sessions of yoga practice [for accumulating gnosis][23] are supported by the six levels of meditative absorption of the form realm [the first absorption level being subdivided into irreversible preparatory, basic, and special absorption states; see section 6.4.1], or even by one-pointed concentration while in the mode of mental functioning of the desire realm. Subsidiary practices are supported by the mental level of the desire realm.

Basic moral practice deals with proper and improper physical and verbal behavior. Sessions of yogic practice deal with the body, and so on, as objects of the meditations on repulsiveness, or as objects of the four foci of awareness. Subsidiary practices involve understanding the words and meanings of the scriptures. 6.A

The Sanskrit term for accumulation [*sambhāra*] denotes the dual accumulation of merit and gnosis, and path means the process of attending to the factors conducive to liberation. The disciples meditate on the faults of the compulsive aggregates that make up the body, such as sickness, sores, and so on, while practictioners of the great vehicle cultivate antidotes for the compulsory nature of the aggregates by realizing their lack of inherent identity.[24]

---

[22]The meditations called the four foci of recollection, the four real efforts, and the four bases of supernormal powers belong to the thirty-seven enlightenment-oriented practices (see section 8.16).

[23]The two accumulations of merit and gnosis constitute the dual stores of personal power.

[24]In the *Compendium of Illuminating Science* (Part 2, "Ascertainment of the Truths") Asaṅga gives this definition:

The accumulation path is manifestation by an ordinary individual of pleasure in morality, control of sense faculties, moderation in eating, in the yogin's diligence of not sleeping during the earlier and later periods of the night, and in memory and self-awareness.

Application Path

The application path provides access to the liberative process that concludes the general practices aimed at experiencing uncondi-tioned gnosis, which were initiated on the accumulation path. Thus, some elements of the application path are carried over from the accumulation path and some are new. These elements unique to the application path are meditation practices leading to direct realization of the four truths and the egolessness of persons and identitylessness of things, which are not "accumulated." It has three degrees of strength: the weak degree is not certain to lead into the insight path, the moderate degree is certain, and the strong degree leads into the insight path in the present life.

There are four phases of the process of realizing [voidness]. They are called warming, peak, tolerance, and highest mundane state. The warming phase is produced [by application of the two accumulations in meditation] and is the precursor of uncondi-tioned gnosis of the insight path, just as the warmth produced by rubbing two sticks together is the precursor of fire. [The Sanskrit term *prayoga* may be translated as "joining" or "putting together."] The Sanskrit term for "peak" [*mūrdhi*] also means crest or point. It is the crest or culmination of the unstable spiritual assets, and it is said that once the peak phase is attained these assets cannot be lost. It also has the sense of "point" because it is very brief. The tolerance phase is elimination of the fear of voidness. The highest mundane state is so called because it is the highest of all mundane mental states and is the uncontaminated controlling causal factor [*causa efficiens*] of the insight path. These phases are also called the "four phases conducive to penetration" because they lead to penetration, or direct realization, of the four truths experienced on the insight path.

The objective of the warming phase is defined in *The Compen-dium of Illuminating Science* as realization "of the [four] truths by the individual himself." This means that the four truths are objects to be realized on the strength of the individual's own meditation and not through the teachings of other people. These objects are the *formulated* [conceptualized] truths, not the *unformulated* [actual] truths themselves. The warming phase consists of preliminary "fore-tastes" of actual realization or unconditioned perception of inherent objective identitylessness of things. Its main elements are concentration and wisdom: one-pointed attention to the objectives by the power of concentration and clear insight free of elaboration [of the objectives] by the power of wisdom, assisted by the other three powers of faith, effort, and awareness. Thus, the mental components of the warming phase are the cognitions and mental functions associated with these five powers.

The objectives of the peak, tolerance, and highest mundane phases are the same as the warming phase. The peak phase is intensification of the preliminary insights [of the warming phase], the tolerance phase is partial penetration [realization] of voidness and its aftereffects, the highest mundane state is realization of the inherent subjective identitylessness.[25] Their main elements are also concentration and wisdom, and their mental components are the cognitions and mental functions associated with concentration and wisdom. The various systems of the lesser and great vehicles differ in their tenets concerning the realizations of these four phases. **6.B**

Concerning level or mode of mental functioning, the application path is supported by the six absorption levels of the form realm: the irreversible preparation, the basic and special states of the first absorption, and the actual absorption states of the second through fourth absorptions. A person who hasn't removed the desires of the desire realm utilizes the preparation level of the first absorption, whereas those who have use the basic absorption state. The antisocial solitary buddhas use the fourth absorption level, whereas the social solitary buddhas use any of the six levels they find convenient. Some schools hold that bodhisattvas utilize the

---

[25]The objective lack of an inherent nature of a personal ego is defined as the lack of inherent nature of the objectively perceived components that are the basis of the illusion of a personal ego. The subjective lack of inherent nature of a personal ego is the lack of inherent nature of the subject itself, the erroneous mind perceiving a personal ego. Likewise, for phenomenal identities the objective and subjective lack of inherent nature are the objectively perceived world and the erroneous mind that perceives the identities of those objective things.

fourth absorption level; others say that they utilize whichever of the six levels they find convenient. **6.C**

There are different theories about the nature of the cognitions comprising the four phases, **6.D**, but I consider them to be direct apperceptive cognitions involving the three wisdoms [derived from learning, reflection, and meditation], which are no different, for example, than apperceptive cognition involving desire.[26]

Insight Path

The insight path is the liberative process that provides access to the realm of reality through direct experiences of voidness. "Insight" [darśana] implies unconditioned perceptions of the real nature of things for the first time. It is the initial occurrence of a mode of mental functioning unconditioned by mundane patterning and is thus the beginning of the "Superior" practice. It is not merely temporary suppression of such patterning, but elimination of their automatic readout in cognitive functioning. Thus it is called "untainted."

The general nature of negative mental functions is disturbance of cognitive operation, and the insight path deals with those which are conditioned since birth.[27] There are the six primary

---

[26]This is somewhat incorrect. Apperception, in those systems that accept it, is simply the self-awareness inherent in every direct or inferential cognition. It is simply self-awareness of the mind; it is not itself aware of the object, since that would incur the problem of an infinite regress of subjects and objects. The cognitions of the application path, however, are aware of an object (i.e., one of the components of the four truths), and thus cannot themselves be apperceptions. Sakya Pandita was correct in the earlier paragraph when he explained that the term "clear insight" was just used conventionally to express a clear inferential understanding (anumāna) of voidness, as when fire is correctly inferred from smoke. Later, upon attainment of the insight path, that same voidness is cognized by direct yogic perception (yogi-pratyakṣa). The significance of this distinction is that the latter has the power to eliminate any afflictive thing it is directed toward, whereas the former, being merely inferential, does not.

[27]Afflictions are either conditioned from birth or innate. The former are eliminated by the process of the insight path and the latter by the transcendent meditation path.

negative functions of attachment, hatred [aversion], ignorance, pride, doubt, and wrong ideas, and their associated subsidiary functions that are eliminated when the primary functions are eliminated. Wrong ideas are of five types: the belief in a personal ego, extreme materialistic or nihilistic beliefs, believing wrong ideas superior, believing that wrong moral and behavioral practices are superior, and wrong views about action [karma] and liberation. [28] 6.E

The insight paths of the disciples, solitary buddhas, and bodhisattvas have certain differences. The disciples believe that the insight path is merely a process of elimination of negative functions, but the more common belief is that it involves production of antidotes that eliminate their corresponding negative functions. The unique view of the great vehicle is that both these ideas are incorrect, since in reality both negative functions and antidotes do not exist:

> There are no "objects" of clear cognition,
> No "thing" that has an identity.
> Things-in-themselves, correctly viewed,
> Are the liberating experience of reality. (EW)

Even on the relative level, it's incorrect to say that negative functions are removed by their antidotes, because when a particular negative function "exists" its antidote does not, and as soon as its antidote is produced, the negative function is gone. The two

---

[28]The five categories of wrong ideas are:

1. The view of ego existence: the belief that the five psychophysical constituents (aggregates) constitute an independent, self-sufficient, permanent ego.
2. Extremism: materialistic or nihilistic views.
3. View conceit: the belief that one's own mistaken view is superior to that of others.
4. Moralistic or ritualistic self-righteousness: the belief that one's own moral practice and religious rituals are the exclusive means of liberation.
5. Wrong views: the denial of the cause-and-effect relationship of action (karma) or of the possibility of liberation or enlightenment.

can't coexist. "Elimination of negative functions" is a conventional way of expressing the experience of direct, unconditioned
cognition. It's like the changing positions of a balance.

The three systems also differ regarding the mental state from
which the insight path can be produced. Since the insight path
involves integration of tranquilization and analytic insight,[29] it
can't be produced from the ordinary mental state of the desire
realm because its preponderance of distractions makes for weak
tranquilization, nor can it be produced from the mental states of
the formless realm where analytic insight is weak. A bodhisattva
produces the insight path from the extremely pure mental state of
the fourth absorption. [See below, section 6.4.1.]

Concerning the objectives of insight meditation, the disciples
attempt to realize personal egolessness, the solitary buddhas
realize the *objective* lack of inherent identity of both persons and
things, and bodhisattvas realize the *subjective* nonexistence of
persons and things. The Illuminating Science Scriptures describe
the removal of three types of conceptual patterning: patternings
for the concept of own existence as a living being, for the concept
of things that compose one's self, and of both patternings with
regard to everything. Asaṅga states in his *Compendium of Illuminating Science*:

> After finalizing the essentially beneficial, mundane factors
> conducive to penetration [on the application path], the first
> state of mental freedom from weak negative conditionings,
> which are part of the things to be eliminated [by insight] is
> produced by insight into the objective of removal of the
> cognitive patternings for one's own existence as a sentient
> being. Then, the second state of mental freedom from moder-
> ate negative conditionings, which are part of the things to be

---

[29]Analytic insight has been likened to the illuminating flame of a lamp and
tranquilization (concentration) to the lamp's windscreen. When tranquilization
is weak, the flame of analysis will be unsteady, blown about by the emotional
afflictions and distractions. Thus development of tranquilization through concentration practice is a necessary prerequisiste to practice of analytic insight.

eliminated, is produced by insight into the objective of removal of the cognitive patternings for things that are constituents of one's own self. Then, the third state of mental freedom from the strong negative conditionings that are to be eliminated is produced by insight into the objective of removal of the conditioned patternings for all phenomena. This constitutes the insight path.

This explanation is based on the common tenet that elimination of conditioned patternings proceeds from weakest to strongest. The unique tenet of the great vehicle, expressed by Nāgārjuna and Āryadeva in accord with *The Mother of Conquerors Sutras*, is that there are no gradations in the realization of voidness. This also applies to common systems proposing that production of the insight path involves a sequence of sixteen cognitions. According to Vasubhandhu, the first fifteen cognitions constitute the insight path and the sixteenth is the "resultant condition." The Differentiators school of the lesser vehicle describes the sixteen cognitions as tolerance toward realization, actual realization, tolerance toward postrealization, and the actual postrealization state for each of the four truths; the tolerances being unobstructed phases and the realizations being liberation phases of the insight process.[30] Other common systems propose eight, four, or just one, and even some great vehicle systems propose that the sixteen cognitions occur very briefly as a single phase. But the unique great vehicle tenet is that the insight path is not actually produced.

> Birthlessness is the single truth,
> and some believe that there are four.
> But beneath the bodhi-trees [Buddha] realized
> No "truth" really exists; how could there be four? (CS)

Nāgārjuna stated in *The Sixty Reasons*:

---

[30]The tolerances are unobstructed phases because they lead directly into the realization phases, which are phases of freedom from the things being eliminated (usually the wrongly perceived inherent nature or qualities of an object).

Ascription of particular characteristics,
Like entrance to realization of things,
Implies production [of the insight path],
Inexperienced persons with such views
Don't understand occurrence from conditional causes.

This doesn't contradict scriptural statements that the insight path is produced through a sequence of sixteen cognitions, or one, or whatever, because these were spoken from the viewpoint of the lower schools that accept the existence of phenomena. But in reality, things are merely dependent happenings:

Not from itself, not from something else,
Not from both, yet not causelessly;
All things whatsoever
Are always uncreated. (EW)

Dependent happening is not production, as stated in *The Sutra Requested by Anavatapta*:

Whatever occurs through conditional causes is uncreated,
It doesn't have a created identity.
Dependent happenings through conditional causes are void,
One who realizes voidness is awakened.

Nāgārjuna explains this further:

I don't reject the conventional expression
"This occurs through dependence on that,"
But since dependent happenings have no self-identity,
How can they be said to "exist"?

There's not a single thing
That is not a dependent happening,
And thus not a single thing
That is not void. (EW)

Meditation Path

The term "meditation path" refers to advanced developmental practices providing access to special concentration states. There are two distinctively different meditation paths: the mundane path consists of practices for attaining levels of meditative absorption [and is not properly included in the five paths] and the transcendent path is the continuation of insight processes begun on the insight path.

The Mundane Meditation Path

The mundane meditation path consists of advanced concentration of practices for producing the eight levels of meditational absorption, which are more refined modes of mental functioning than that of the desire realm and provide the mental stability, clarity, and attentional control necessary for insight practices. [These concentration practices are also called "tranquilization."] The eight absorption levels consist of the four absorption states of the form realm and the four mental equanimities of the formless realm.

Preparatory Concentration Practice.   During earlier stages of practice, each absorption state results from preparation concentration practice consisting of a seven-step system of attentional deployment performed while in the next lowest mental level. For attaining the first absorption state they are as follows.

The first step is comparing the modes of mental functioning of the desire realm and the first absorption. Through the wisdoms derived from learning and reflection produced while in the mental level of the desire realm, one realizes that it has many negative mental functions that agitate the mind and produce misery and short lifespan, and that the higher mental levels are better. This produces the mental clarity and one-pointed focusing of attention on the first absorption state, and by these one understands the mental courseness of the desire realm and the relative tranquility of the first absorption level.

The second step is intensification of the foregoing practice, which leads to the exclusive concentration on the first absorption with wisdom derived from meditation, which surpasses the previous concentration involving the wisdoms derived from learning and reflection.

The third step is further analysis through concentration as before, which suppresses the overt operation of negative desire realm mental functions by producing antidotes for the stronger negative functions removed by wisdom derived from meditation.

The fourth step is called "increasing bliss" because the bliss of suppression of coarse negative functions and the bliss and lesser ecstasy arising from isolation [from sensory stimuli during concentration] are experienced and seen to be beneficial. This produces an intermittent concentration embued with strong confidence [in the effectiveness of practice], which is the antidote for moderate-strength negative functions.

After thus suppressing most desire realm negativities, the fifth step, called "thorough examination," is an analytic concentration in which negativities are allowed to arise in order to determine whether all negative functions have been removed and whether suppressed negativities will reoccur.

This examination leads to the sixth step of "conclusive practice" in which you see that some negativities can still occur, and thus you go on to produce antidotes for subtle negativities by meditation on the relative coarseness and tranquility [of successive mental levels] as explained earlier.

The seventh step is called "result of conclusive practice" because it is attention to the experiential results of the meditation process just described and leads directly [into the mental state of the first absorption]. This same seven-step method is used to attain the second absorption level, and so on up to the eighth.

Suppression of negative mental functions proceeds from strongest to subtlest. The steps of further analysis, increasing bliss, and conclusive practice are the antidotes for strong, moderate, and subtle negative functions, respectively. From the viewpoint of their function in the process of attaining absorption states, the steps of comparing the modes of mental functioning, then intensifying that practice are the application phase; the steps of further analysis, increasing bliss, and conclusive practice are the unobstructed phase; thorough examination is the special phase; and attention to the results of practice is the freedom phase.[31]

Actual Absorption States.   The eight absorption states are characterized by specific alterations in cognitive functioning. Since they are all tainted [by conditionings], they are mundane mental states. The first four are of the form realm. The first absorption state has two levels: a basic absorption state where the cognitive functions of scanning and resolution [which produce the patterning of conditioned cognitions][32] and the bliss and ecstasy resulting from isolation from sensory stimuli are present, and a special state where the scanning function is absent. The second absorption is a state of concentration having both bliss and

---

[31]The mundane meditation path has four phases for suppressing the afflictions. The application phase is a tentative suppression, the unobstructed phase is actual suppression, the freedom phase is the succeeding state of freedom from a particular affliction, and the special phase is the examination for other afflictions to apply the above three phases to them. In general, when dealing with mundane meditation practices, the application phase leads to attainment of a tolerant state, which itself leads to realization while on the transcendent meditation path; the unobstructed phase (also called the tolerant phase) is freedom from blockage to realization; the special phase is repetition of this process; and the freedom phase is the result. The four similarly named phases of the transcendent meditation path have the distinction of eliminating afflictions and their traces, not merely suppressing or preventing their manifest occurrence.

Weak degree phases suppress (or eliminate) strong afflictions because they are coarser and more easily recognized and removed. Likewise, weak afflictions are the most subtle and difficult to recognize, and are more pervasive: thus, they require a strong degree phase to remove them. Suppression (or elimination) proceeds from strongest afflictions to weaker afflictions, because strong afflictions disturb the mind more and mask the weaker ones. The mind must first be tranquilized by their removal to the point where the weak ones can be detected and dealt with.

[32]Scanning and resolution are two of the so-called "variable" mental functions. They function in the second and third cognitions of an object, following the initial direct cognition by a sensory process, to roughly scan the range of appropriate concepts and names and then resolve that down to a precise, clear mental image.

ecstasy, but the third has only ecstasy. In the fourth absorption both bliss and ecstasy are absent; it is a concentration of pure mental neutrality.[33] The four absorption levels of the formless realm are extremely refined states of mental equanimity produced by certain meditations during the special phase [the "thorough examination" step] of preparatory practice. The equanimity of infinite space is produced by meditating on all things as merely space, and space as infinite. The other three equanimities of limitless consciousness, blankness, and neither-aware-nor-unaware [which is also called "pinnacle of existence"] are produced in a similar way.[34]

Absorption states are considered tainted if they have the negative mental functions of craving, wrong attitudes, pride, and ignorance. If they are undisturbed by these negative functions, they are called "purifying absorptions," because they are beneficial to spiritual development. A bodhisattva's absorption states are especially untainted because they are produced through practice of transcendent meditative absorption and include advanced concentration practices such as "warrior's stride" and "level crossing." An absorption state can be unstable, stable, special, or conducive

---

[33]In his *Compendium of Illuminating Science* Asaṅga gives the characteristic mental functions of these absorption states as follows:

> The first absorption has five characteristic mental functions: scanning, resolution, bliss, ecstasy, and mental one-pointedness. The second absorption has four: clarity (consisting of recollection, self-awareness, and affective neutrality), bliss, ecstasy, and mental one-pointedness. The third has five: affective neutrality, recollection, self-awareness, ecstasy, and mental one-pointedness. The fourth has four: pure affective neutrality, pure recollection, neutral feeling, and mental one-pointedness.

[34]The four levels of the formless realm are also called "media" because the media (i.e., sense faculties and their objects) of such persons have the following characteristics:

1. Media vast as space
2. Media vast as consciousness
3. Null media, which is the same as nonawareness
4. Media neither with nor without conception (i.e., unclear weakly functioning conceptual processes)

to penetration [realization of voidness]. In the lesser vehicle these are interpreted as tending to degenerate back to the lower level, self-maintaining, conducive to attaining the next higher level, and supporting the insight path. The Mind Only school of the greater vehicle holds that an unstable state has a preponderance of negative functions but does not degenerate from that absorption level, a stable state tends to be self-maintaining, a special state supports special spiritual assets like clairvoyance, and so on, and the fourth state is capable of supporting the superior paths [the insight and meditation paths]. Thus they are bases for the application, unobstructed, special, and freedom phases [of the liberative processes of those paths].

The utility of these concentration practices is that they suppress the tendencies for negative mental functions and are supportive of beneficial assets, like the four infinitudes and five supernormal abilities, and also of the superior paths of insight and meditation.

The Transcendent Meditation Path

[The term "meditation path" is somewhat misleading here, since all five paths involve meditation practices.] The Sanskrit term *bhavana marga* might be better translated as "cultivation path," because it is the process of cultivation or further development of the direct experiences of the realm of reality initiated on the insight path. This process has four phases, the application, unobstructed, freedom, and special phases, and the methods of practice consist of cultivation of actual realization experiences and their postrealization states.

The cognitive patternings or conditionings eliminated by the transcendent meditation path are the *innate* patternings that produce concepts of personal ego and separate identities of phenomena, which in turn prevent pacification [of the subtlest negative mental functions]. There are sixteen types: the innate elements of the six primary negative functions of the desire realm [attachment, hatred, ignorance, pride, doubts, and wrong ideas], and the five each in the form and formless realms, where hatred is naturally absent. * Further, when each of the sixteen primary ones are divided into strong, moderate, and subtle, there are 414 subtypes of innate cognitive patternings, and also 414 corresponding types of antidote. You should refer to the explanation of the method of elimination by antidotes in the previous section dealing with the insight path [section 6.3].

Production of the Meditation Path. The practices of the disciples, solitary buddhas, and bodhisattvas are different. The disciples' meditation path is produced while in the mental state of one of the absorptions of the form realm, including the preparation and special states of the first absorption, or in the three lower equanimities of the formless realm. The other mental states are not suitable because the mind of the desire realm is not refined enough, the mind of the "pinnacle of existence" [eighth absorption level] is not sharp enough [because it is too tranquil], and the preparatory concentrations for the second to seventh absorptions are too weak in tranquilization because of the effort expended in trying to attain the next higher level, which makes unification of tranquilization and the analytic insight impossible. Although the preparation for the first absorption level is also weak in tranquilization, it can support the meditation path because it involves less expenditure of effort. Social solitary buddhas produce the meditation from any mental state of the form realm, whereas the asocial solitary buddhas use the fourth absorption state. Bodhisattvas produce the meditation path from the extremely pure fourth absorption state.

Regarding the methods and objects of meditation, both vehicles consider it to be further meditation on the absolute reality of the four truths following the insight path, in which tranquilization and analytic insight are both present. The great vehicle has the unique tenet that it is meditation cultivating the unification of the extreme opposites of absolute reality experienced on the insight path with the clear perception of phenomenal reality.

---

*The Compendium of Illuminating Science lists only ten types because it is based on a different canonical scripture [The Untangling the Knot Sutra], with a less detailed itemization—SP.

Final Path

The final path, sometimes called "path beyond practice," is the conclusive process that provides access to the realm of reality. There are three types: that of the disciples, of the solitary buddhas, and of the bodhisattvas. The disciples consider its dependence on mental level to be the same as the transcendent meditation path, and both vehicles hold that solitary buddhas and bodhisattvas attain it in human lives through the adamantine concentration supported by the fourth absorption level. The great vehicle has the unique tenet that it is attained on the tenth bodhisattva stage through the controlling causal factor of the adamantine concentration based on the extremely pure limit of the fourth absorption level.

The disciples' adamantine concentration suppresses subtle latent propensities of the afflictions during its application phase and eliminates them entirely during the unobstructed phase. Bodhisattvas' adamantine concentration suppresses the subtle propensities of both afflictive and cognitive obscurations during the application phase and eliminates them entirely during the unobstructed phase. This amounts to saying that disciples and solitary buddhas realize conditioned nirvana, whereas bodhisattvas realize *unconditioned* nirvana, which is perfect enlightenment. Both vehicles hold that adamantine concentration is direct perception of the four truths, or the truth of cessation, or the ten dharmas beyond practice. The latter are right speech, action and livelihood comprising the morality group, right concentration and awareness comprising the concentration group; right views, thinking and effort of the wisdom group; as well as right liberation and right liberative insight, which is subdivided into transcendent gnosis of the unconditioned state and pure mundane postrealization state.

Other terms for the final path [*niṣṭhāmārga*] are "path beyond practice," because it is conclusive elimination of all afflictions and realization of all objectives, "uncontaminated root virtue," because it is uncontaminated, and "conclusive eliminative antidote" because the eliminated afflictions will not reoccur. **6.F**

7

The Stages of Development

Prior to his attaining the insight path, the stages of a bodhisattva's practice are considered "mundane" and correspond to the stages of "practice by determination" of the accumulation and application paths. These are the bases of spiritual assets conducive to realization of voidness and attainment of the insight path. The actual "ten bodhisattva stages" commencing with attainment of the insight path are thus called "transcendent." Their general characteristic is that they are the bases for *special* spiritual qualities of superior beings on the insight, meditation, and final paths.

The ten bodhisattva stages consist of seven impure stages called Joyous, Immaculate, Illuminating, Radiant, Hard to Master, Confrontation, and Far Reaching, and three pure stages called Immovable, Superintellect, and Cloud of Dharma. The concept of "purity" refers to the strong pride on the seven impure stages, and the absence of pride on the three pure stages. The ten stages can be correlated with the transcendences, the first six stages corresponding to the six transcendences and the last four stages to the four additional transcendences of method, strength, supplication, and gnosis.

Bodhisattvas on these ten stages attain spiritual assets of freedom, such as crossing the four rivers of misery:

Superior beings are completely free
From aging, sickness, and death;

They are free of them because their births
Are not compelled by action and afflictions. (PP)

They also free themselves from anxiety about maintenance of
life, untimely death, dishonor, lower rebirth, and harm from evil
persons. The degree of freedom increases greatly from stage to
stage, and you should understand that although bodhisattvas are
free from the aforementioned things, they *evince* miseries of birth,
aging, sickness, and death by voluntarily taking birth in samsara
in order to help others.

Having seen reality as it really is,
They've transcended birth and death,
But out of compassion they voluntarily take on
Birth, aging, sickness, and death.

They also gain the assets of skill in concentration and meditative absorption, meeting buddhas and receiving their blessings,
perceiving and visiting many worlds and buddha realms, developing many beings and opening the manifold doors of Dharma,
being present in many eons and thus knowing the past and future,
and producing manifold emanation bodies. These assets increase
from stage to stage and are described in greater detail, along with
other assets, in works like *The Sutra of the Ten Stages*, *The
Untangling the Knot Sutra*, *The Crown of Great Vehicle Sutras*, *The
Bodhisattva's Stages*, and *The Digest of the Great Vehicle*.

The Sanskrit word for stage [*bhūmi*] means ground or place,
implying that the stages are the ground for the gradual upward
climb to liberation. Names for each stage are explained in *The
Crown of Great Vehicle Sutras*:

Nearer to enlightenment,
Fulfillment of beings' welfare in sight,
Great joy arises,
Thus that stage is called Joyous.

Untainted by immorality
[The second] is called Immaculate,

And because it sheds much light on Dharma
[The third] is called Illuminating.

Blazing with the fire
Of enlightenment-aimed practices
That consume both [obscurations]
The [fourth] stage is called Radiant.

Because concern for others' development
And protection of one's own mind
Are hard to reconcile, even for the skillful,
[The fifth] is termed Hard to Master.

Since the experience of transcendent wisdom
Leads to the conflict of dualistic perception
Of samsara and nirvana, the [sixth]
Is called Confrontation.

Since it links [pure and impure] stages
Into one journey, the [seventh] is Far Reaching,
And because one is unswayed by concepts
[The eighth] is called Immovable.

The stage of Superintellect is so-called
Because of mastery of analytic knowledge:
On Cloud of Dharma, [apparent and void] realities
Interpenetrate like clouds in the sky.

I've met many people who think they can attain enlightenment without progressing through the five paths and ten stages, or
that they can experience the voidness of the insight path without
the precursory accumulations of merit and wisdom. But such ideas
are not found in any of Buddha's sutras or tantras. The goal of real,
perfect buddhahood is attained by traversing the five paths and ten
stages; the five paths culminate in a buddha's dharma body and the
ten stages in the form body. For the five paths, the efficient cause is
generation of the *absolute* intent for enlightenment through
cultivation of wisdom, the direct realization of voidness, and the

subsidiary causal factor is compassion, the actualization of skillful methods. Conversely, the efficient cause for the ten stages is generation of the *relative* intent for enlightenment, which involves compassion and skillful methods, and the subsidiary causal factor is realization of voidness.

8

Enlightenment

The final result of buddhist practice is "supreme enlightenment," the attainment of all spiritual potentialities, both ordinary and unique. A buddha is a person who has realized *"unconditioned nirvana"* and is thus free from samsaric conditionings through transcendent wisdom and freed from the limitations of conditioned nirvana through compassion. A buddha is *"the* Teacher" who demonstrates the real possibility of unconditional freedom, which unlike the disciples' nirvana is not just cessation of misery and personal existence, but a state of freedom from which one can help others reach that goal.

Buddhahood is characterized by total eradication of the afflictional and cognitive obscurations along with their latent traces, a completely undistorted perception of both the unmodified void and the apparent aspects of things simultaneously. A buddha has three "bodies" or modes of being. The essential body is the natural purity of the inherent element of reality and freedom from the adventitious taints of conditioned existence. The perfect enjoyment body exists in the supraworldly realm ["*Akaniṣṭha* heaven"] and has the thirty-two major and eighty minor physical features of a superior being, a voice that continually spins the wheel of Dharma, a mind endowed with the four spontaneous gnoses [see

below], and an audience of bodhisattvas in all stages of development receiving its teachings. A buddha's emanation bodies derive
from the enjoyment body and take birth any place in the universe
where there are beings in need of guidance, working continually
for their welfare. There are three types of emanation body: prebirth
emanations residing in Tuṣita heaven prior to being born into the
world as supreme emanations, which are the historical buddhas
like Śākyamuni, and "artificial emanations" created for specific
purposes.

The three bodies can be condensed into two: the "reality
body," which is a reflection of absolute reality, and the "form body,"
which includes the enjoyment and emanation bodies existing on
the level of superficial reality. Some scriptures divide them into
four by calling the essential body the "reality body," and calling the
unification of the three bodies the "essential body." But since this is
mainly found in the tantric system, I won't discuss it here.

Concerning a buddha's unconditioned perception, there is
some confusion among the various systems. Some hold that
unconditioned perception [gnosis] is an existent function of a
buddha's mind, arguing that without functional perception a
buddha would be a lifeless automaton, activated only by prior
accumulation of merit and gnosis, and enlightenment would be no
different than the disciples' nirvana. Others, such as the Mind
Only system, argue that it cannot actually exist because then a
buddha's cognition would be conditioned by perception of the
apparent aspect of things and would have subtle ego clinging
because of the subjective aspect of such perception. Actually, this
boils down to the question of whether a buddha actually "exists."
My system handles this on both absolute and superficial levels. On
the absolute level a buddha's cognition is free from the extremes of
existence or nonexistence because it transcends the ordinary
mind's dualistic perception of "objects."

No "thingness" exists in true nirvana.
Since it doesn't exist, [nirvana] doesn't [actually] exist.
Philosophers espouse "existence" or "non-existence,"
But by such speculations misery will not be stilled. (KC)

On the superficial level, unconditioned perception cannot be an existent function of a buddha's mind because of elimination of the fundamental error of dualistic perception, and yet in view of a buddha's omniscience it must exist because of the transformation gnoses, as described by Candragomin:

> The basic process [*ālayavijñāna*]
> Becomes mirrorlike cognition,
> With the natural clarity
> Of the reality element.
> Transformation of negative mental functions
> Is termed "equivalence cognition,"
> Transformation of consciousness itself
> Is termed "discriminative cognition,"
> And transformation of the five sensory processes
> Is the "[cognition] achieving all aims." (SB)

The unification of the superficial and absolute aspect constitutes a buddha's unconditioned liberation. According to Nāgārjuna:

> When samsara and nirvana,
> After being understood separately,
> Are truly integrated—
> This is called "unification."

While experiencing voidness, one is temporarily free from conditionings, definitively realizing "thatness" [and suppressing the apparent aspect of things]. Afterwards, while developing what was experienced, one develops skill in methods in order to eliminate the seeming contradiction between appearances and voidness. Finally, the two are conclusively unified in unconditioned liberation. A buddha's cognition is free from subject-object duality; and, in fact, this freedom from dualistic mentality is achieved by transformation of the dualistic mentality itself. This is the reason for the term "mirrorlike cognition." Likewise, equivalence cognition, which realizes the equivalence of one's self and all other beings and things, is transformation of negative mental functions into realization of inherent equivalence free from the conceptual patternings that differentiate self and other. The transformations of ordinary mental functionings into the transformation cognitions is more fully explained in works like *The Proof of Others' Mental Continuum*, *The Achievement of Gnosis*, and *The Crown of Great Vehicle Sutras*.

A buddha has both common and unique spiritual qualities. I will explain them according to *The Crown of Great Vehicle Sutras*, but since that work leaves some out, I've added additional material in order to provide a compendium of the qualities of enlightenment.

The Four Infinitudes

The first three infinitudes are a buddha's intentions of happiness: the love that desires that all beings be happy, the compassion that wishes they be free from misery and the joyful wish that happiness and freedom from misery be not denied them. The fourth infinitude is neutrality, the helpful intention of eliminating the affliction of attachment to happiness and aversion to misery. [See section 4.5.]

The Liberations and the Suppression and Saturation Concentrations

The eight liberations such as viewing the material, and so on, are freedoms from attachment achieved by elimination of mental obscurations. Disciples and solitary buddhas eliminate the emotional obscuration but not the latent traces of the negative emotions or the cognitive obscuration, whereas a buddha is totally liberated from both obscurations and their latent traces.

The eight suppression concentrations are absorptions wherein certain aspects of one's conceptual representations of external things are temporarily suppressed. Ordinary persons can, at best, suppress appearances in the immediate environment, disciples and solitary buddhas can suppress a much wider range, and a buddha can suppress the whole universe.

The ten saturation concentrations are alterations of the perceptual processes involving visualization of material things or qualities to make them appear in the form of earth, water, red, blue, and the like after suppression of their usual appearance. Ordinary persons, at most, can extend this just within a small range. Disciples have a larger range, and a buddha can extend such visualization to all perceivable things.

Freedom from Negative Emotions and Attitudes

The disciples are involved only in themselves and thus eliminate only the overt forms of their own negative mental functions, not their latent propensities. A buddha has not only removed his own negativities and their latent traces, but he also subdues the negativities of other beings, helping them generate their own antidotes through his mercy for afflicted beings.

Intentional Knowledge

The disciples' intentional knowledge involves effort and concentration. It is therefore limited, unable to cut through all doubts. A buddha's intentional knowledge is spontaneous, unattached to things and unobstructed by them. It is always impartial and able to cut through the doubts of all questioners.

The Four Types of Analytic Knowledge

Analytic knowledge of things enables an enlightened person to explain the basis of things and analytic knowledge of meaning enables him to explain the significant characteristics of those things. Analytic knowledge of etymology enables him to explain the essential meanings of scriptural terms, whereas self-reliant analytic knowledge enables him to understand the knowledge embodied in the scriptures.

The Six Types of Superknowledge

The superknowledge of miraculous physical emanation is the ability to be present anywhere there are trainees. The supernormal ability of mental articulation allows penetration of the minds of beings. The supernormal ability of revelatory speech provides understanding of their individual languages through divine hearing. A buddha's arrival from previous lives is made possible by the recollection of all past existences, the departure from this life and the transmigration to the next through divine sight of death and rebirths, and the eventual emergence from samsara through knowledge of the cessation of contamination. An enlightened person endeavors to remove delusion by giving advice in accord with this knowledge.

The first five are contaminated and can belong to unenlightened people, but the sixth is uncontaminated and possessed only by those "beyond practice."

Divine sight is clairvoyance that results from the four meditative absorptions of the form realm, and, since it requires perfect and pure absorption states, it is very pure. The things perceived through clairvoyance include the deaths and between-life existences of other beings and whether they are headed for happy or unhappy rebirths.

Knowledge of the cessation of contamination means elimination of all latent propensities, possession of the uncontaminated mental antidote, and a mind imbued with supreme wisdom. Such an unconditioned mind is liberation; such wisdom is liberation. Having surpassed the limits of existence through previous meditation of the five paths, a buddha guides others who also want to realize things-as-they-are for themselves. He guides them by means of the superknowledge of the cessation of contamination, clearly demonstrating he has attained it. Thus he urges them to "experience it for yourself in this life through this superknowledge: then communicate it to others."

The Fourfold Purity

The fourfold purity consists of four abilities. Purity of support accomplished by the total elimination of all latent propensities is the ability to take up any body, abide in it as long as needed, and leave it at will. Purity of objective is the ability to manifest what doesn't exist and transform what does. Purity of mind is skill in all types of concentrations through the accumulation of virtue and elimination of all negative conditioning. Purity of gnosis is unobscured perception of all things through elimination of ignorance.

The Ten Strengths

They are:

1. Knowing what is beneficial and harmful.
2. Taking responsibility for one's own actions [karma].
3. Knowing the various dispositions of trainees.
4. Knowing their types of motivations.
5. Knowing their capacities.
6. Knowing the omnipresent path [literally "the path that begins everywhere"].
7. Knowing the relevant relationships of the five powers, five strengths, seven enlightenment factors, eight liberations, the concentrations, equanimities and positive and negative mental factors.
8. Knowing previous lives through recollection.
9. Knowing death, transmigration, and rebirth by divine sight.
10. Knowing the cessation of contamination.

The ten strengths are thus presented from the viewpoint of

their function but they can also be expressed as the conquering of the deceptions that delude beings with regard to these four goals:

Deception in method—belief that higher existence and liberation may be obtained by practices like sacrificial offerings or jumping into rivers—is corrected by knowing what is beneficial and harmful. By understanding the relationship of cause and result, you know that only virtue is conducive to higher rebirth.

Deception in refuge means belief that just paying respect to God, Visnu, and so on, without accumulating merit or even by doing what is sinful, will preserve you from lower rebirth. This is corrected by taking responsibility for your own actions.

Deception in purity—belief that contamination can be removed by ablutions, austerities, and so on—is corrected by the strength of knowing the relevant relationships of the meditative absorptions, concentrations, and equanimities that constitute the real path to purification.

Deception in emergence—teaching paths not in accord with the trainee—is corrected by the remaining seven strengths. The strength of knowing the capacities of trainees enables an enlightened person to teach dharma appropriate to their degree of faith, effort, recollection of prior existence, concentration and wisdom. Likewise, knowing their types of motivation refers to their degrees of aspiration and realization; and knowing their dispositions refers to the component elements of their psychophysical make-up, inclinations, desires, and so on. The omnipresent path is the knowledge of the appropriate practices for each trainee to enter the path. Recollections of former lives means recalling the characteristic of all types of being, specifically, the eight basic facts of name, species, race, requirements, state of happiness or misery, birth, lifespan and end of that life, and various secondary qualities.

The Fourfold Fearlessness

An enlightened person has no fear when among prideful, worldly people and outshines them all when teaching about the four obstacles to their own and others' welfare. This arises from the fearlessness of knowing how to teach and knowing that he is omniscient, free of misery, and free of delusion.

Undefensiveness

Because of the purity of physical, verbal, and mental actions, he or she is relaxed among companions, without anxiety about being accused of faulty behavior. Outshining them all, he speaks out the dharma; and although some trainees follow his teaching success-fully while others try but are unsuccessful, and still others accom-plish little because of their particular abilities, a buddha is free from any favoritism because of this.

Conquest of Latent Propensities

Disciples and solitary buddhas often neglect others' welfare through forgetfulness, but a buddha has obtained the result of continual, consistent performance in teaching his method to anyone, in any land, at any time, in any way, for any purpose, without wasting time.

Great Compassion

This means constant, impartial dedication to helping beings whether they are degenerating, developing, emerging from lower existences, and so on.

The Eighteen Unique Properties of a Buddha

Six of the eighteen unique properties of a buddha are activities: (1) A buddha uses his body flawlessly. Arhats sometimes walk in front of elephants or carts, fall into bramble pits, are bitten by stepping on snakes, or wander into rooms designated for the opposite sex, but a buddha does none of these. (2) He or she eschews unnecessary speech. Arhats sometimes make unnecessary sounds and noises when alone, but a buddha does not. (3) A buddha is mentally equanimous at all times. Arhats will leave the state of mental equanimity and enter the postrealization state, but a buddha has unified equanimity and postrealization and never shifts from one to the other. (4) His memory never fails. A buddha is not forgetful in speech or deed. (5) He does not believe samsara and nirvana are different. He does not think that the samsara is only misery and nirvana only happiness, because he has realized the equivalence of samsara and nirvana. (6) A buddha achieves his mental neutrality through analysis, so he lacks the unanalyzed mental neutrality of the arhats. Since their cessation equanimity is unanalyzed (i.e., retains latent propensities), they sometimes neglect the welfare of beings. A buddha never does this.

Six of the unique qualities involve realization: (7-12) Since arhats haven't eliminated the cognitive obscuration, they are still subject to degeneration of aspiration, effort, recollection, concentration, wisdom, and liberation. A buddha is not subject to such degeneration.

Three involve gnosis: (13-15) An arhat has obstructions and attachments connected to events past, present, and future, but a buddha's gnosis is free from this.

Three involve action: (16-18) Although arhats are involved in virtuous physical, verbal, and mental actions, it is sometimes productive only of the eight absorption levels. Since a buddha's actions are directed by gnosis, preceded by gnosis, and imbued with gnosis, they are always in accord with gnosis.

Omniscience

With a dharma body naturally pure and free from adventitious taints, with the perfect enjoyment body to teach the great vehicle continually to bodhisattvas of the ten stages in Akaniṣṭha heaven, and with the three types of emanation bodies, a buddha works continually for beings' welfare, cutting through all their doubts. He perceives things-as-they-are and things-as-they-appear simultaneously and uses this realization to achieve his own and others' welfare.

Accomplishment of the Six Transcendences

A buddha is unselfish in giving, is without lapses of morality, patient without anger, and energetic without pause caused by laziness. His meditative absorption is unmoved by distractions, and his wisdom is free from mental fabrication toward all things.

The Thirty-Seven Enlightenment-Oriented Practices

The four foci of recollection (realizing the body and other things to be like space, and so on), the four real efforts (exertion in order to eliminate faults, prevent their occurrence, produce and increase their countermeasures), the four bases of miraculous powers (the extensive concentrations imbued with aspiration, effort, mental stabilization, and judgment), the complete five powers and the corresponding five strengths (faith, recollection, effort, concentration, and wisdom), the seven enlightenment factors (recollection, penetration of things, effort, bliss, practiced intensity, concentration, and affective neutrality), and the eightfold superior path (right views, right thought, right speech, right action, right livelihood, right effort, right mindfulness, right concentration).

The Equanimities

The nine equanimities involve elimination of preconceptions associated with the three realms, from the grossest to the most subtle. The preconceptions associated with the desire realm are

eliminated upon entrance into the equanimity of the first absorption level and, likewise, for the remaining three absorption levels
of the material realm and the four media of the immaterial realm.
When all preconceptions associated with the three realms are
eliminated, one enters cessation-equanimity. [See section 6.4.2
on the mundane meditation path.]

The Three Doors of Liberation

The three doors of liberation are voidness through freedom from
subject-object dualism, desirelessness through freedom from attachment to the five compulsive aggregates, and signlessness
through eradication of conditioned conceptualization. Although
the disciples and solitary buddhas do indeed possess these three
doors, they haven't eliminated the final obscuration of latent
propensities.

Triumph over the Four Devils

The root of superior gnosis is wisdom by means of which a buddha
conquers the devil of affliction through realizing the inherent
nonexistence of a personal ego, which causes afflictions. By means
of this realization a buddha then conquers the devil of the
aggregates by freeing the aggregates of compulsiveness; and the
devil of death is conquered by freedom from the inevitable linkage
of one life to the next, inherent in compulsive aggregates. With
the strength of love, the root of compassion, a buddha conquers
the devil—son of the gods, stilling all destructiveness through
viewing every being as if it were an only child.

The Ten Powers

The first of the ten powers is power over lifespan—remaining in
the body as long as desired. Power over mind is the ability to enter
whatever mental state is desired, and power over necessities is the

ability to get all necessary things. These powers result from earlier practice of giving.

Power over action is intentional control of physical, verbal, and mental action, and power over birth is the ability to choose any incarnation. Both of these powers result from earlier practice of morality.

Power over determination is the ability to transform earth into gold and so on, the result of having motivated other beings by means of patience.

Power over supplication is the ability to fulfill the aim of any helpful intention, which results from having worked for the welfare of others by means of effort.

Power over miracles is the result of having understood the intentions of all buddhas by practicing meditative absorption.

Power over gnosis is unconditioned perception that results from working for the welfare of beings by means of wisdom.

Power over dharma is the ability to teach whatever type of dharma is needed.

Concentration

A buddha has unobstructed, effortless concentration in all activities that is unexcelled. This includes developmental concentrations like "warrior stride," "jeweled throne," and "lion's stance," and the eliminative concentrations like the "adamantine" and the "total elimination of affliction." These are extensively treated in *The Mother of Conquerors* literature.

The Door of Mantric Speech

Through the door of mantric speech he opens the gate of all dharma, as in *The Inexhaustible Basket Sutra*, which gives the mantra "Om Mani Padme Hūm." All conceivable syllables of the Sanskrit alphabet are all contained in the seed syllable "Āh," and by his understanding of this he can comprehend others' beliefs in the course of teaching them.

Elimination of the Two Obscurations

He is free from all obscurations because he has eliminated the afflictional obscuration—the contamination or "taints" such as attachment and hatred—and the cognitive obscuration—the limited concepts of the three spheres of self, field, and objects, along with all their latent traces.

Unconditioned Cognition

Mirrorlike cognition is the foundation of help for others. The first perceivable things like the reflection in a mirror. Equivalence cognition is freedom from the concepts of "I" and "mine." Discriminating cognition is the treasury of all good qualities like strength and fearlessness. Cognition for accomplishment is the spontaneous accomplishment of all work for oneself and others. Mirror-like cognition is the foundation of help for others. The first three are related primarily toward one's own welfare, whereas the last is primarily for others.

Transformation

The unconditioned gnosis body is attained by transformation of the contaminated elements of the material body. As stated in works like *The Crown of Great Vehicle Sutras* and *The Digest of the Great Vehicle*, all action and afflictions of an ordinary being become the inconceivable gnosis of transformation.

Supreme Refuge

Finally, of all the foregoing qualities, worldly persons may possess the infinitudes, the liberations, the suppressions and saturations, and the first five types of superknowledge. The superknowledge of cessation of contamination, the freedom from affliction, intentional knowledge, the thirty-seven enlightenment-oriented practices, the meditative absorptions, the three doors of liberation, and so on may be possessed by some of the disciples. Some of the other qualities, some supernormal abilities, concentrations, transformations, and so on, are gained on the first seven stages, the "impure states," of a bodhisattva's ten stages. Transformation of the afflictive mentality, and some of the signs and marks of a great person, are gained on the eighth bodhisattva stage. The door of mantric speech and the four types of intentional knowledge are gained on the ninth stage, and the advanced concentrations and the ten strengths are gained on the tenth. The eighteen unique qualities of a buddha, the fourfold fearlessness, the undefensiveness, and the rest are special qualities possessed only by buddhas, and this makes such a person the holy refuge of the whole world. The teacher with such qualities is none other than the Victorious Buddha. Since his teachings are the source of fulfillment of all needs, they are like a treasury of jewels. Through the merit of this exposition that presents and illuminates them may all beings come to clear perception of all phenomena both as they appear and as they really are.

With clear vision of the import of the scriptures,
Buddha's thought, profound and extensive,
I've illuminated them with helpful intent
According to the teachings of Bodhisattva Maitreya.

In accord with my own teacher's teaching
I've logically taught the Enlightened One's scriptures
With no contradiction between teachings and practice,
And the absolute view of transcendent wisdom.

These days Śākyamuni's teachings, neglected,
Are fading like a dying fire,
Thus you intelligent seekers of freedom
Should attend to Muni's words with care.

Common people are wrong
About the subtle thatness of things;

By my words and those of your teacher
May you recognize wrong ideas and end them.

Buddha's lamp has dimmed in this world,
Skillful teachers are hard to find,
Thus Buddha's teachings are ruined these days
By stupid, unpracticed, ignorant people.

To explain dharma wrongly is a heavy sin
When well-explained people are offended.
It's hard to teach dharma in degenerate times;
But try to have helpful thoughts toward others.

Make a commitment right now
Toward this and all other good deeds:
"May I attain the station of Omniscient Conqueror
To fulfill the needs of beings to the limits of space."

Colophon

This text of the graduated practice of the bodhisattva path, titled
Illuminating Muni's Thought, was written by Sakya Pandita, up-
holder of Buddha's scriptures. I have composed this compendium
of Dharma for everyone in central Tibet and for all the world. Now
that you, my disciples, have obtained empowerment, you should
study this text, teach it, and practice accordingly.

This English translation was completed by Geshe Wangyal
and Brian Cutillo in Washington, New Jersey.

PART TWO

Notes by
Sakya Pandita

Notes by Sakya Pandita

Chapter Two: Starting Practice

2.A   There are different ways of understanding the Three Jewels. The disciples and solitary buddhas don't accept Buddha's triple body; they believe that the Śākyamuni who attained buddhahood at Bodhgaya is the only Buddha. They don't accept the great vehicle as authentic Dharma; they accept only the scriptures of the disciples [the Pali canon]. They don't accept the Community of bodhisattvas, but only the disciples' eight types of realized persons. The followers of the great vehicle accept Buddha as having the triple body, the great vehicle as authentic Dharma, and the Community as consisting of bodhisattvas.

The Three Jewels of the secret teachings are also different. [They are great bliss, voidness, and their unification,] but I won't explain them here.

2.B   Some people think that accepting medical treatment indicates lack of confidence in Dharma, and thus taking medicine is harmful to one's refuge vow. However, in the section on medicine in the Discipline Scriptures it is stated that a sick [person, even a] monk should have medical treatment and medicine. In fact, since diet is one of the four types of medical treatment, just eating and drinking would be harmful to one's refuge! So how could taking medicine be harmful? Intelligent people find this idea ridiculous! [It is based on the mistaken notion that taking refuge in the Three Jewels implies not relying on anything else, but taking refuge really means relying on the Three Jewels as the only *ultimate* refuge; it's not wrong to rely on a doctor curing sickness, and so on.]

2.C   Once a woman donor, giving a cotton robe to a senile old monk, requested Dharma from him. Being unable to explain any Dharma he was desperate, and repeated over and over, "I am miserable because of my ignorance." The donor joyfully realized from this that ignorance is the cause of misery. Scholars praised him, saying, "He is liberated from the ocean of worldly misery."

Then a robber thinking to steal the robe followed him. When the fool entered his house, the robber shouted, "Give me your robe!" Because of his fear the old man would not come out, so he said, "Take it through the window." But when the robber reached for it with one hand, the old man said, "The donor gave this to me respectfully, with two hands. You also must take it with both hands." When the robber reached in with both hands the old man bound them with rope and tied it to the centerpost of the house. He then went outside and beat the robber with a stick, shouting the refuge formula to each of the Three Jewels with each stroke, and then sent him away.

The robber was crestfallen and went to sit by a river. A passing traveler asked him, "Why are you sad?" "I am a robber," he replied, "but a monk is a better thief than me. He beat me with a stick with each line of the refuge formula. Buddha in his omniscience arranged the refuges as three, yet now even I know on my life that there isn't a fourth!"

Having said this with faith in Buddha, he crouched in the water under a bridge. Thereupon a troop of demons tried to cross the bridge, but were unable. "Previously we could easily cross this bridge. What is the reason?" they asked the robber.

"You yourselves are very clever. As for myself, I know only the

refuge in the Three Jewels. Other than that I know nothing." It is
said that even those demons came to an understanding of refuge
and were reborn as gods. Also, the robber became a monk through
his faith in Buddha.

Chapter Three:
The Intent for Enlightenment

3.A   The former are the practices of the disciples, the solitary
buddhas, and the actual, perfect Buddha. In the great vehicle, the
system of the Mind Only school derives from the teachings of
Maitreya and Master Asaṅga, and is explained in *The Twenty Vows*
[by Candragomin], which is based on Asaṅga's masterwork *The
Bodhisattva's Stages*. The system of the Middle Way school derives
from the teachings of Mañjuśrī and Master Nāgārjuna, and is
explained in Śāntideva's *Entering the Bodhisattva's Practice*, which
is based on *The Wreath Sutra* and the practices of Jetari, and the
like. These systems differ in certain particulars, such as the marks
of a teacher, rituals, and specific instructions. For a detailed
explanation of the rituals and instructions of the Middle Way
school, you should refer to my own text *The Ritual for Production of
the Intent for Enlightenment of the Middle Way School*.

3.B   [Example of debate on the question of whether the absolute
intent for enlightenment is "produced."] One might argue, "The
passage on the acts of worship on the *Vairocana Abhisaṃbodhi* that
gives a formula for production of the absolute intent for enlightenment contradicts what you have said."

The *Vairocana Abhisaṃbodhi* is a *caryātantra*, where the term
"production of the absolute intent for enlightenment" is assigned
to the mantra for compiling the accumulation of wisdom. But in
the system of the transcendences (*pāramitāyāna, mahāyāna*) there
is no explanation of a ritual for production of the absolute mind.

It is not correct to mix the texts of the different tantra systems,
the yoga and *anuttarayoga* tantras, and likewise it is not correct to

mix the texts of the secret tantric instructions with the production of the absolute intent of the system of transcendences.

"As meditation involves thought constructs it is opposed to the *mahāmudrā*, which is free of thought constructs."

Well, as ritual is superficial it is opposed, by similar argument, to the absolute nature of the production of the absolute intent. Therefore, those fools who don't know the levels of tenets and tantras misunderstand their import by making the fundamental error of taking a mere name at face value.

The direct answer is that it is always necessary to differentiate between explicit and implicit meaning in dealing with the four systems of tenets and the three vehicles. Concerning the different systems, the generated intent for enlightenment is considered absolute in the lesser vehicle and superficial in the great vehicle, whereas in the secret teachings the absolute mind production can be meditated as having even form and color. The term "absolute intent" is assigned even to voidness meditation by terms like "voidness," "freedom from all existents," and so on. Designations like "moon" for the superficial and *vajra* for the absolute are immeasurable. These additional reasons should also be understood.

Do not confuse the ritual of the secret teachings with the generation of intent of the vehicle of transcendences. In the sutras and sastra texts, the rituals for production of superficial aspirational and functional intent for enlightenment are thoroughly explained, but nowhere in the sutras and sastra texts is the production of the absolute intent explained. This is especially true of the Middle Way school of Master Nāgārjuna, *Entering the Bodhisattva's Practice* of Śāntideva, and so on, but a ritual for production of the absolute intent is likewise not mentioned in the scriptures of the Mind Only school of Master Asaṅga, *The Twenty Vows*, and the works of Atīśa.

You might ask, "Although it is not mentioned, if ritual is performed with inner aim how would it be contradictory?"

If it were produced *from* the ritual there would be a contradiction, for the absolute would seem to come from superficial generation of intent. Also, all sutras state that one obtains tolerance toward birthlessness; I haven't heard anything about obtaining tolerance to birth. What greater confusion could there be than ritualizing what is without ritual, degrading the absolute to the level of the superficial, treating the unborn as born, expressing the inexpressible, and imagining the unimaginable? As it says in *The Ornament of the Sutras*:

> One who doesn't see what exists, and sees what doesn't
>   exist,
> What can be done with such a blind man?

The logic of this passage is that someone with a clouded eye is unable to see forms that exist, but sees nonexistent things such as hair before the eyes and a white shell as yellow. Likewise, those fools who don't comprehend the classifications of the scriptural divisions that elucidate dharma, or the profound rituals of empowerment and the like, meditate the deities of the secret teaching for production of the aspirational and functional intent for enlightenment that is nowhere mentioned, and perform rituals of text recitation for production of the absolute intent. Such things were nowhere mentioned by Buddha and are harmful to the teachings.

3.C   Concerning death in general, it is caused by exhaustion of lifespan, exhaustion of good action [karma], exhaustion of merit, combinations of these two, or all three. Exhaustion of lifespan can be ameliorated by the rituals of longevity from *The Tantra for Eliminating Lower Births*, prayers to Vijayā, and the like. Exhaustion of action [karma] is ameliorated by saving an animal from slaughter, preserving a life from certain death, protecting someone from harsh punishment, and so on. Exhaustion of merit is reversed by the constructive conditions of guru worship and services to the Three Jewels that restore merit. That is, worshipping Buddha, reciting Dharma texts, gathering together groups of the Community, making offerings to demons, renunciation as the antidote for desire and the like, medicine as the antidote of illness, proper perception [of the path] as the antidote of mind, blessings and causal conditions to aid all beings, and so on.

In the event of two simultaneous exhaustions, repair whichever two are exhausted: lifespan and action, or lifespan and merit, or action and merit. These three double exhaustions can be repaired only with great effort. When all three are exhausted, there is no method of reparation and one will die. Like smoke from an extinguished fire or a pond whose source has stopped, even Buddha Bhagavan's prayers will not correct the situation of such a person and he will certainly die. This is the mark of the triple exhaustion.

Thus it is not right to lose faith because a service seems ineffectual. This is like thinking, for example, that if someone dies in bed the bed is at fault, or if he dies in a house the house is at fault, or if he dies after eating and drinking the food and drink are at fault, or if he dies after taking medicine the medicine must be at fault. Similarly, as the real taker of life is the exhaustion, it is not due to the ineffectuality of services or root virtues.

3.D   To explain this further, you should avoid four types of negative behavior and cultivate four types of positive behavior, as explained in *The Heap of Jewels Sutra*: "Four behaviors obstruct the intent for enlightenment. What four? Deceiving your teacher and holy persons, making others feel guilt undeservingly, not respecting and praising those who have really entered the great vehicle, and falsely pretending to have the 'special intent' while actually treating others badly. Four behaviors will assure continuity of the intent for enlightenment throughout all future lives. What four? Not telling lies intentionally, living sincerely and honestly, according to the special intent, regarding all bodhisattvas as your teachers and praising them to the ten directions, and inducing those who are mature enough to strive for real enlightenment by convincing them of the limitations of the lesser vehicle."

3.E   This is more extensively explained in *Good Practice*, *The Bodhisattva's Confession of Lapses*, *Maitreya's Supplication*, Master Nāgārjuna's *Twenty Verses*, and Master Śāntideva's *Entering the Bodhisattva's Practice*. If you have difficulty handling this material you should use *The Seven Branches* by my own teacher or my own book, *Ten Dharma Practices*. Also you can read about the various examples of a bodhisattva's deeds in the *Birth Stories*.

3.F   *THE HUNDRED SYLLABLE MANTRA:*

OM VAJRASATTVA, SAMAYAMANUPĀLAYA
VAJRASATTVA, TVENOPATIṢṬHA
DṚDHO ME BHAVA, SUTOṢYO ME BHAVA
SUPOṢYO ME BHAVA, ANURAKTO ME BHAVA
SARVA SIDDHIM ME PRAYACCHA,
SARVA KARMAṢU CA ME, CITTAM ŚRĪYAM KURU
HŪM! HA HA HA HA HOḤ!!!
BHAGAVĀN SARVATATHĀGATA VAJRA
MĀ ME MUÑCHA ! VAJRĪ BHĀVA!
MAHĀSAMAYASATTVA ĀḤ HŪM PHAT!

Chapter Four:
The Six Transcendences

4.5.A   The disciples' preliminary practices are reflection on the repulsive aspects of the body for persons with excessive emotional attachment and meditation utilizing the counting of breaths for those with excessive mental conceptualization. Actual absorption meditations consist of the thirty-seven enlightenment-oriented practices included in the five paths: the four foci of memory on the accumulation path; the four right efforts in the warming phase for the application path; the four bases of supernormal powers in the peak phase: the five powers in the tolerance phase and the five strengths in the supreme mundane phrase; the eightfold superior path on the insight path; and the seven enlightenment factors on the meditation path [see sections 6.4 and 8.3].

4.5.B   Concerning the benefits of producing compassion, *The Crown of Great Vehicle Sutras* states:

Bodhisattvas are free of misery:
They are freed from misery by misery;
Initially afraid of it,
When it happens they are blissful.

This means that while on the level of practice by determination [prior to realizing voidness], they have anxiety about the practice of compassion that involves exchanging their own happiness for others' misery. This arises from their ignorance of the actual nature of the practice of equivalence of self and others [see discussion in text, below]. Later, on the stage of pure intent [the first of the ten bodhisattva stages], they experience the great bliss of tolerance when confronting pain.

4.6.A   The four [Indian] systems with materialistic views are the Vedic, Sāṃkhya, Vaiśeṣika, and Jain; the nihilistic view is held only by the Carvakas. The four materialistic systems accept a permanent ego that is bound to samsara by action [karma] and emotional afflictions and attain liberation [moksa] when released from them. The nihilistic Carvaka system accepts an existent ego that is neither bound to samsara nor capable of being liberated from it.

4.6.B   Further, with regard to attaining buddhahood, the nirvana of the disciples and solitary buddhas [which is the goal of this practice] is an even greater straying than the lowest rebirths.

> Birth in hell
> Is not a final obstruction to enlightenment;
> Disciplehood and solitary-buddhahood
> Are final obstructions to enlightenment.

And from *The Heap of Jewels Sutra*:

> Once when Śāriputra was teaching dharma, five hundred monks attained arhatship. Because of their poor realization they no longer respected the subtle dharma spoken previously by Ārya Mañjuśrī and thus fell among the beings of the fire hells. Śāriputra said to Mañjuśrī, "You have done an intolerable action." Mañjuśrī replied, "Indeed, Śāriputra, that is so. I have done an unbearable action."
> Then Śāriputra told Buddha, "Mañjuśrī has done an intolerable action."

Buddha replied, "How?"

"When I explained dharma, five hundred monks attained arhatship, but thanks to Mañjuśrī's Dharma teachings they fell into the fire hells."

Buddha replied, "Indeed, Śāriputra, when you explained dharma they became arhats, but then they would have been continually without the fortune of enlightenment. By Mañjuśrī's dharma teaching they will spend awhile in hell, but when liberated from there they will quickly attain manifest, perfect buddhahood. Thus Mañjuśrī is skilled in method."

Therefore, disciplehood and solitary buddhahood are great strayings. The sutras, tantras, and śāstras all reject them.

4.6.C Huashang composed such books as *The Wheel of Sleep Meditation*, *Message of Meditation*, *A Further Message*, *The Backside of Reality*, and *The Origin of the Eighty Sutra Sections*. Since his teachings didn't agree with the Indian system of Buddhism, the king invited the Indian master Jñānendra to find the truth about the Indian and Chinese systems. Jñānendra told him, "Master Śāntarakṣita's last words were, 'In the land of Tibet nonbuddhist teachings will not flourish because of the twelve dharma protectors recruited by Padmasambhava. However, there will grow together side by side, day and night, month by month, a pure and a corrupt dharma. After my death a Chinese teacher will arrive who will reject method and wisdom. His school will be called 'Mere Blankness Is Sufficient,' and it will claim that buddhahood is attained by merely realization of mind. Buddha said, 'In the five degenerate ages, in the one called Degenerate View, people will delight in 'voidness.' Not only in Tibet, but all people of the five degenerate ages will be overly attracted to voidness as the only dharma. If this spreads, it will be harmful to Buddha's teachings. At such a time you should invite my disciple, the skillful Kamalaśīla, to debate the Chinese teacher. The superior system will win. This is my prophecy. I beseech you to do this.'"

So the king invited Kamalaśīla. After assembling a jury of wise men, the king confiscated all weapons and ruled that when either side won, the whole assembly must present the winner with their flower garlands, respect him, and abandon the loser's system.

Anyone not doing so would be punished. Siding with the king were just a few adherents to the Indian system like Lonpo Go, whereas those siding with the Chinese teacher were many—the queen herself, Jang Chub, Si Mel, Ba Jo, Ma Ma, and so on.

During the debate once of the exchanges went as follows:

Kamalaśīla asked, "What is this Chinese system?"

The Chinese teacher replied, "Your system that progresses gradually upward from the taking of refuge and production of intent for enlightenment is like a monkey climbing to the top of a tree. In my system buddhahood is not attained by means of action and agent, but by direct realization of mind through meditation without thoughts. It is a practice descending from above, like a garuda bird descending from the sky to a treetop. This is Mere Blankness is Sufficient."

Kamalaśīla replied, "Your example and its meaning are both faulty. I begin with the fault of the example. Was your garuda bird born in the sky with developed feathers and wings before it descended to the treetop, or was it born on the ground and then gradually developed wings and feathers with which it could ascend and then descend? The former, a sky-born bird, doesn't exist and the latter is not a correct example of instantaneousness, but rather an example of gradualness!"

The Chinese teacher couldn't reply, and Kamalaśīla continued, "Not only is your example faulty, but its meaning is also wrong. What is this meditation without thought? It must be either partial stoppage of thought or complete stoppage of thought. If you say that it is partial stoppage, then sleep, unconsciousness, and the like would be thought-free meditation since they involve partial stoppage of thought.

"On the other hand, if you say that it is complete stoppage of thought, such a thought-free state must either proceed or not proceed from a *thought* to meditate without thought. If it does not so proceed, then all beings of the three realms must be producing this meditation because it is produced without the prior thought to meditate! And if it proceeds from the thought to meditate without thoughts, the intent to meditate without thought is ruined since that is a thought. For example, a person who says, 'I have taken a vow of silence,' spoils his vow."

He refuted him further with scripture and reason. At this the Chinese teacher was helpless. The king said, "If you have an answer, give it!"

The teacher replied, "Since it's like a lightning bolt in my head, I don't know how to answer."

The king said, "As this is so, I request you all to present your flower garlands to the Indian master. The 'Mere Blankness Is Sufficient' system doesn't agree with scripture and reason. You must follow the Indian system. Hereafter anyone following the Mere Blankness Is Sufficient dharma system will be punished."

He made this law over all Tibet and collected the Chinese teacher's books in the repository of Samye monastery. The Chinese teacher returned dejected to China, expressing this prophesy to his disciples, "One of my boots was left in the debate hall as a sign my teachings will overcome the Buddha's teaching there."

Another version has it that the Chinese teacher, head in flames, faced west, toward Sukhāvatī, and died. His followers Ba Jo and Ma Ma beat themselves and leaped to their deaths. There are many such stories, but I won't write them here; you should look them up in *The King's Good Explanations*.

4.6.D   It is a mistake to meditate a voidness without realization of the two egolessnesses. The skillful have stated, "They are mistaken." It is predictable that they will be angry at those who meditate real voidness.

You might think, "It is indeed incorrect to meditate merely according to the Mere Blankness Is Sufficient system. But if one first meditates the preparatory taking of refuge, production of the intent-for-enlightenment, personal deity and lama, placing the mind in the actual state of *mahāmudrā* and dedicating the outcome, practictioners of the Mere Blankness Is Sufficient system would then be superiors [Ārya]." Let's examine this. If you meditate this transcendence you must know the profound and extensive meanings of the six transcendences, thirty-seven enlightenment-oriented practices, and so on, cut through presumption concerning the subjective and objective self-naturelessness through the medium of listening and reflecting, understand thoroughly the personal phenomenal egolessnesses, and don the armor of giving hands and feet, and so on, through three immeasurable eons. If you practice thus according to the system of the Five Maitreya texts and the like, this will indeed be transcendent wisdom. But since the system you suggested isn't explained in any sutras or sastra texts it isn't transcendent wisdom.

The real *mahāmudrā* of the secret teachings involves initiatory empowerment and the concentrations of the two [tantric] stages of development [i.e., developing stage and fulfilling stage]. If you don't first obtain the initiatory empowerment for tantric practice that develops beings; don't know the meditations of the two stages of tantric practice; don't realize the aim of *mahāmudrā* derived from these two stages; never know how to meditate with mental elaboration, without mental elaboration, and extremely free of mental elaboration; and fail to traverse the stages of inner dependent occurrence—you are not practicing the *mahāmudrā* as explained in the secret teachings. Such meditation cannot avoid the extremes of samsara and nirvana, just as with small pebbles you cannot bridge the Ganges. To avoid the two extremes of samsara and nirvana you must bridge them with the good masonry of the six transcendences and two stages of the secret teachings. Therefore, no matter how good a meditation may be, if it isn't explained in either the transcendence literature or secret teachings it isn't a meditation associated with those two.

Or again you might think, "Buddhahood is not attained by any dharma of action and agent. The very thought to meditate without attention is itself thought activity and thus not actual *mahāmudrā*. It is, however, the method for producing *mahāmudrā*." Since the thought to meditate without thought is itself a thought activity, it contradicts the statement that buddhahood isn't attained by any dharma of action and agent. It is not correct to say that absence of thought can be produced merely by the thought to meditate without thought. It is as if you could cure illness merely by thinking, "I will be free of sickness." What can be said of such a belief? Just as a special diet, medicine, and the like are the cause of curing an illness whereas merely thinking, "I will be free of sickness," is not, likewise the accumulations of merit and gnosis are the causes of preconceptionless concentration, whereas the mere thought to meditate without thought is not.

4.6.E You might think, "All inner and outer things are recognized as lacking inherent identity instantaneously." At the time of actual realization, experience arises through "production" of voidness, but during the post-realization state various mental patterings [conditionings] and thus various objects—visible, sounds, and the like—are again experienced. These manifold occurrences occur neither through causes nor causelessly. Self-production is the Sāṃkhya system and production through a different cause is held nonbuddhist Maheśvara system, the disciples' system, or any system accepting existence of things. Causeless production is a nihilistic belief. Such wrong ideas can't be rejected without scripture and logic, and thus there can be no realization without the wisdoms derived from learning and reflecting on scripture and logic. To produce wisdom derived from meditation, it is necessary to stop presumption by means of the wisdoms derived from listening and reflecting, and only when thoroughly practiced in this can the illuminations of the wisdom derived from meditation occur.

Nowadays I've seen many people claiming to have wisdom derived from meditation, but their teachings contradict scripture and logic. Their books contain many explanations with incorrect terminology and many analyses that disagree with scripture and logic. In debate they can't even distinguish between former and latter terms in a proof! I've seen ridiculous debates where the contestants don't even know the proper conditions for acceptance and rejection in a proof! Such faults cannot be claimed to be wisdom derived from meditation. The sutras state that this is wrong realization and corrupt wisdom.

Therefore, you must stop presumption by listening and reflecting and then meditate the correct meaning free from doubts.

4.6.F *The Sutra Demonstrating the Nonorigination of All Things* says:

After the parinirvana of the Everestlike Tathagata Abhyudgatā Rāja incalculable eons in the past, the dharma succession fell to a monk named Pure Deeds. At that time, there was another monk named Wise Deeds of extremely pure morality who had obtained the five mundane superknowledges, possessed many spiritual qualities such as extensive practice of the discipline, and who devoted himself to meditative absorption and solitude.

"The dharma teacher Pure Deeds, together with his disciples, came to stay at the temple where Wise Deeds lived, but out of mercy and compassion for beings went repeatedly to the villages where many thousands of people had faith in him. Although he had attained enlightenment, the monk Wise Deeds didn't have faith in this bodhisattva. So he beat the sandalwood plank to assemble the Community of monks, and ordered them, 'You are staying at my place. No one is permitted to go to the villages. You are acting without critical awareness and talking too much! Why are you going to the villages? The Bhagavan himself stayed in monasteries and praised this. You must not visit the villages but should practice the bliss of meditative absorption.'

"But they did not heed him, and again went to the villages. Wise Deeds beat the sandalwood plank again and assembled the Community of monks. He told them, 'If you go to the villages after this, don't return to this temple.'

"In order to save the mind of that monk, the dharma teacher Pure Deeds called his disciples together and told them, 'None of you go to the villages.' But the people who were being developed by these monks were unhappy and lost their impulse for virtue. After three months the monks again left the temple to visit the villages, towns, and even the king's palace to teach Dharma. Wise Deeds saw the dharma teacher Pure Deeds going to the villages again and again, and believing that his followers were ordinary people, had the same attitude as before. He told many people, 'This monk has corrupt morals and indulges in social pleasures,' thus turning them away from hearing dharma.

"Through the results of this action, after Wise Deeds died he suffered millions of eons in the hell of unceasing torment. For sixty lives he was unable to hear or speak. For 32,000 lives he was unable to keep his vows. For many hundreds of thousands of lives he had weak faculties.

"Nobly born, at that time the monk Wise Deeds was me myself. The dharma teacher Pure Deeds, by the root virtues of explaining dharma and upholding the buddha doctrine, attained buddhahood in the Eastern Joyous Field of Akṣobhya."

4.6.G Some people say that the two realities lack a common ground because there is nothing common to both realities. This is incorrect. Although there is nothing in common in the objects when classified as either superficial or absolute, the fact that they are merely different modes of cognizing the same things is non-contradictory from the viewpoint of negation of opposites [*anya-apoha*].[35] As Candrakīrti stated in *The Commentary on the Sixty Verses of Reasoning*, "The classification of the two realities is done from the viewpoint of mundane cognition."

4.6.H The disciples hold that "cognitions of ordinary individuals are superficial, the equanimity states of the three superiors [disciples, solitary buddhas, and bodhisattvas] are absolute, their postrealization states are superficial, and nirvana is exclusively

---

[35]"Negation of opposites" (*anya-apoha, gzhan sel*) is a logical technique established in the epistemological system of Dignaga. It reflects the view that conceptual knowledge is derived from the elimination of opposites. That is, "cup" is identified by elimination of "non-cup." In cognitive psychology this is equivalent to memory search by means of a "pruning tree" strategy. This basic aspect of buddhist epistemology arises not only from the requirements of a logical system of knowledge theory (*pramāṇa*), but also from the process of conceptual learning and perception. The function of words and concepts is not viewed as affirmative, as they might seem, but to a negation of errors or wrong possibilities, as explained in Dharmakīrti's *Exposition of Valid Cognition*.

The application of logical "negation of opposites" to the question of sameness or difference of the two realities can be understood by considering the example of a product (compounded phenomenon) and its impermanence. Every product, or compounded thing, is indeed impermanent; their range is identical over the range of phenomena. But they are not identical on the level of concepts—the word "products" does not automatically produce the concept "impermanent," and vice versa. Therefore "product" and "impermanent" are said to be essentially identical, but different negations of opposites (*ldog pa tha dad*). The expression "different negations of opposites" refers explicitly to their difference in the conceptual realm. Although Sakya Pandita does not explain this application of negation of opposites to the two realities, he indicates this stance by emphasizing that the superficial and absolute realities are simply different modes of cognizing the same thing. Superficial reality is perceived by a mundane, nonanalytic cognition, and absolute reality is known by its unfindability in any analytic, mundane cognition, and of course by direct perception in a transcendent cognition by wisdom. (Adapted from Leonard Zwilling, *Dharmakīrti on Apoha*, University of Wisconsin, University Reprints, 1976.)

absolute." This is incorrect because in their system nirvana is accepted as substantially existing and thus cannot be [absolute]!

The Mind Only school holds that "the imaginary nature is superficial, the relative nature impurely perceived is superficial, the relative nature purely perceived is absolute, and the perfect nature is exclusively absolute." But this isn't correctly the absolute, since only the nondual mind contacts the ultimate nature of a thing [and thus relative nature purely perceived cannot be the absolute].

The Self-Proven Middle Way school holds that "each of the two realities can be certified or uncertified, making a total of four types. An appearance in the unanalytic cognition of an ordinary individual is uncertified superficial. Reality in an analytic cognition is certified absolute. The preconceptionless gnosis of the three Superiors is uncertified absolute. Pure mundane gnosis is certified superficial." Although it's not wrong to say that a buddha's gnosis exists, however it does transcend both existence and nonexistence [in its perception of things] and thus cannot be divided into preconceptionless gnosis and pure mundane gnosis. Such duality exists only in the mentality of the 'near-sighted.' From *The One Hundred Thousand Verse Transcendent Wisdom Sutra*:

> "Samsara" and "nirvana"—
> Those with insight accept them,
> Those who see don't accept
> The duality of samsara and nirvana.

4.6.1 If you know how to explain this from the viewpoint of negation of opposites [*anya-apoha*] no fault will be incurred, but if you don't know you will be unable to avoid the faults previously stated. Therefore, in our system it is considered on two levels: the absolute level and the level of verbal conventions. On the absolute level they are free from all mental fabrications of sameness and difference, as stated in *The Untangling the Knot Sutra*:

> Superficial world and absolute thatness
> Are characterized by lack of sameness and difference

Whoever understands them as same or different
Entertains an erroneous view.

On the level of verbal conventions they are treated only according to such statements as, "From the viewpoint of negation of opposites they are the same thing but different opposites," and "They cannot be expressed as same or different."

4.6.J To explain the etymology of the terms, "superficial" in sanskrit is *saṃvṛti*: *sam* means "completely," *vṛ* is the root of *āvaraṇa* and means an obscuration or covering. Thus, it means completely obscuring or covering absolute reality. The earlier Tibetan translators, however, rendered it as *kun rdzob*, meaning "totally essenceless" or "spurious," and this was never rectified.
  "Absolute" is *paramārtha*. *Parama* means "superior" or "ultimate." *Artha* means "object." Thus, since it is the ultimate object when examined by superiors, it is called absolute.

4.6.K A given thing that is a cognizable object is superficial in nature; its perceivability in a nonanalytic cognition is verified by an apperceptive direct perception [*svasaṃveda-pratyakṣa-pramāṇa*]. A specific thing that is not a cognizable object, however, is absolute in nature, since it is not perceived to exist in an analytic cognition. How is it verified? If this specific thing were verified, wouldn't this contradict its transcending cognizable objects? There is no contradiction. Through negation of opposites [*anya-apoha*] it is verified as not being a cognizable object by analysis of cognizable objects, and it is verified as an object by analysis of nonobjects. For example, on ultimate analysis a knowable is found to be not knowable, and this nonknowable when analyzed is verified as knowable. From *The Exposition of Valid Cognition*:

Therefore the terms "knowable," and the like
Are merely verbal conventions;
Only the analytic process exists.

Therefore, since it is not verified directly in a cognition, the absolute is not a knowable [of the mundane mind].[36] Since because of this it transcends cognizable objects, we don't incur the fault of [accepting its] perceivability in [mundane] cognition.

Chapter Six: The Five Paths

6.A   Some people say there is no wisdom derived from meditation on the accumulation path, but this is incorrect. Asaṅga says in his *Compendium of Illuminating Science*: "By cultivating the wisdoms derived from listening, reflecting, and meditating, and other causal virtues, one becomes a vessel that is the basis of realization and liberation."

6.B   The Differentiators school and the Sutra Followers school don't accept any difference in objective or form in the application paths of the disciples and solitary buddhas, and *The Compendium of Illuminating Science* also doesn't explain any difference. Some followers of the great vehicle do accept differences in the application paths of the three vehicles, stating that the disciples' warmth and peak realize the *objective* lack of inherent nature and their tolerance and supreme mundane state realize the *subjective* lack.

---

[36] Tsongkapa, in exposition of the dialectical Middle Way system, does accept that the absolute reality is a knowable of the mundane mind. Although it is known by its unfindability under analysis that eliminates inherent identity from its object, we have seen (note 35) that such elimination of error is a quality of all conceptualization. Thus "unfindability under analysis" is the object of such a cognition and is the mode in which absolute reality is perceived by the mundane mind. After this unfindability is ascertained by analysis it may then be realized by direct perception in a transcendent cognition.

Although in both Tsongkapa's and Sakya Pandita's systems the direct perception of absolute reality (voidness) occurs only on attainment of the transcendent wisdom of the path of insight, Tsongkapa asserts that whether it is known by its unfindability in a mundane analytic cognition or by direct perception in a transcendent cognition, the very same object is being cognized. These two modes of cognizing the absolute also differ experientially—direct, transcendent perception is much stronger and more effective in eliminating afflictions and preconceptions than indirect, analytic cognition.

The solitary buddhas' warmth and peak realize the objective lack of inherent nature and their tolerance and supreme mundane state realize the subjective lack of inherent nature of the personal ego and a portion of the phenomenal egos. The bodhisattvas' warmth and peak realize the objective lack of inherent nature and their tolerance and supreme mundane state realize the subjective lack of inherent nature of *both* personal ego and phenomenal identity.

Others—following the unique intentions of the great vehicle stated in Vasabandhu's commentary on *The Crown of Great Vehicle Sutras* and the intention of the *Sutra chu bo tsha sgo can*—hold that in the bodhisattva's application path, "Warmth is concentration obtaining a preliminary insight [into reality]. Peak is concentration increasing that preliminary insight. Tolerance is concentration partially penetrating the thatness of the object. Supreme mundane state is concentration immediately antecedent [to direct penetration of voidness of the path of seeing]."

Nāgārjuna, however, following the intentions of the transcendent wisdom scriptures, doesn't accept any difference in the realization of egolessness in the application paths of the three vehicles, with the exception of differences in methodology and in clarity of the objectives in the four phases of penetration. His acceptance rests according to such statements as, "Those wishing to practice the disciples' stages should practice this same transcendent wisdom," and, "A person wishing to become a sugata, disciple, solitary buddha, or dharma king will be unable to do so without obtaining the support of this tolerance."

The application path can be produced by men and women of the human world and by the six classes of gods in the desire realm. But the application path can be produced after birth in one of the six classes of the desire realm gods only if the accumulation path has been previously produced in a human existence.

6.C To justify the enumeration, the Sutra Followers school holds that realization of the objective lack of inherent nature is warmth, peak, and tolerance, and that realization of the subjective lack of inherent nature is supreme mundane state. In this system realization of the subjective lack of inherent nature has three degrees: weak is the warmth of obtaining a preliminary insight, moderate is peak increasing that insight, and strong is tolerance, which is its strong realization.

Some followers of the great vehicle hold that warmth and peak realize the objective lack of inherent nature in afflictive things; peak realizes the objective lack of inherent nature in purifying things; tolerance the subjective lack of inherent nature or that lack in the mind perceiving the substantial existence of persons; and supreme mundane state realizes the subjective lack of inherent nature in the mind perceiving the nominal existence of persons. As stated in *The Ornament of Realizations*:

> By basis and its antidote
> The two types of objective realization;
> And by the degrees of such delusion and its eradication
> Nine individual types in all.

> From the viewpoint of perception
> And eradication of an independent ego
> Two types of subject, perceiving
> Substantial and nominal existence, are accepted.

According to the higher and lower Illuminating Sciences (the Abhidharma systems of Asaṅga and Vasubandhu, respectively), the phases of the application path, with the exception of tolerance, are not graduated into weak, moderate, and strong, and the supreme mundane state is instantaneous. *The Treasury of Illuminating Science* states:

> Just as the strong degree of tolerance
> Lasts just one instant, supreme state does likewise.

Thus this is called the "concentration of one session." Some followers of the great vehicle, however, hold that there are twelve in all by dividing each of the four phases conducive to penetration into weak, moderate, and strong degrees. As stated in *The Ornament of Realizations*, "By weak, moderate, and strong . . ." Thus supreme mundane state is held to have temporal extension [in this system]. [This is an incorrect reading of the text of *The Ornament of Realizations*. The supreme mundane state is the instantaneous interface between the tolerance phase and the *insight* path; it always leads directly into the transcendent experience of voidness.]

6.D You might think that this contradicts the explanation of it as a clear insight [in the foregoing quote from *The Eight Thousand Verses*], but it isn't so. It is just a conventional expression of clarity, not of actual direct penetrative perception, as in statements like, "Clear realization of fire by means of inference on seeing smoke," and, "Those monks skilled in the wisdoms derived from listening and reflecting have focused their minds in clarity." Direct perception is unmistaken and free of thought constructs, whereas the phases conducive to penetration are associated with thought constructs, as explained in *The Analysis of the Mean and the Extremes*.

Some people hold that it is mental void based on scripture, but this is not correct. We have already rejected this [by stating that it arises from the strength of the individual's own meditation and not another's teaching]. Others hold that it is mental direct perception [i.e., of the sixth consciousness] and mental identification based on recollective awareness, but they don't even know logic.

What type of cognition are these four phases conducive to penetration?

Some hold that it is direct yogic perception because the commentary on the *The Eight Thousand Verse* [version of the *Transcendent Wisdom Sutra*] explains that during the phases conducive to penetration clear insight occurs. However, if thought constructs occur [as they do on the application path], there cannot be clear insight [i.e., direct perception]. Examine this. If it is just loosely termed "direct yogic perception," let's not quibble over terms, but if you believe it is the real direct yogic perception, it would be the path of seeing! If you feel that the path of seeing is the extending of direct perception over the totality of the dharma element [i.e., voidness] whereas on the application path one cognizes only a part, this would necessitate that the meditation path be the path of seeing since the characteristic of the path of seeing is the seeing of reality not directly realized previously [and the meditation path is its extension to the reality of all things]. Thus the path of seeing is explained as the seeing of reality not directly seen previously, and not as the extending of such direct sight. Some of them even claim that direct yogic perception isn't necessarily superior [i.e., Ārya, occurring only in one who has attained the path of seeing], but they are unacquainted with either scripture or logic.

6.E   They may be divided into those which are eliminated on the insight path and those eliminated on the meditation path. The Vaibashika system holds that there are eighty-eight types of negative mental functions eliminated on the insight path, as explained in Vasubandhu's *Treasury of Illuminating Science*. In *The Digest of the Great Vehicle* Asaṅga proposes ninety-four, but in his *Compendium of Illuminating Science* he gave a total of 112.

6.F   As a footnote to this section, I might add that those who hold the tenets common to [both] the vehicles have the belief expressed in *The Treasury of Illuminating Science* that during the application path a "faculty for the realizing what was [previously] unknown" develops, which is empowerment of the path of seeing; during the path of seeing a faculty for the means of omniscience develops, which is empowerment for the meditation path; and during the meditation path a faculty for possessing omniscience develops, which is empowerment for the final path. The tenets unique to the great vehicle, however, do not even mention such faculties.

List of Works Cited

Numbers preceded by "T" following Tibetan titles refer to *The Tibetan Tripitaka*, Peking edition, edited by Daisetz T. Suzuki. Tokyo-Kyoto: Tibetan Tripitaka Research Institute, 1957. Numbers preceded by "Toh" refer to *A Complete Catalog of the Tibetan Buddhist Canons*, Derge edition, edited by Hakuju Ui, Munetada Suzuki, Yensho Kanakura, and Tokan Tada. Sendai: Tohoku Imperial University, 1934.

1. Buddha's Word (Sutra and Tantra)

Advice to the King Sutra. Rājādeśa nāma mahāyanā sūtra. rgyal po la gdams pa zhes bya ba theg pa chen po'i mdo. T880. Ārya rāj-āvavādaka nāma mahāyanā sūtra. 'phags pa rgyal po la gdams pa zhes bya ba theg pa chen po'i mdo. T881.

The Bodhisattva's Confession of Lapses. Ārya triskandha nāma mahā-yāna sūtra, second section. 'phags pa phung po gsum pa zhes bya ba theg pa chen po'i mdo. T950.

Buddha Wreath Sutra. *See* Wreath Sutra.

Eight Thousand Verse Transcendent Wisdom Sutra. Ārya aṣṭādaśasā-hasrikā prajñāpāramitā nāma mahāyanā sūtra. 'phags pa shes rab kyi pha rol tu phyin pa khri brgyad stong pa zhes bya ba theg pa chen po'i mdo. T732. Translated by Edward Conze: *The Perfection of Wisdom in Eight Thousand Lines & Its Verse Summary*. Bolinas, California: Four Seasons Foundation, 1973.

Epitome of Thatness Sutra. Sarvatathāgata tattvasaṃgraha nāma mahā-yāna sūtra. de bzhin shegs pa thams cad kyi do kho no nyid bsdus pa zhes bya ba theg pa chen pa'i mdo. T112.

Epitome of Transcendent Wisdom. Ārya prajñāparamitā sañcayagatha. 'phags pa pha rol tu phyin pa sdud pa tshigs su bcad pa. T735. Translated by Edward Conze: *The Perfection of Wisdom in Eight Thousand Lines & Its Verse Summary*. Bolinas, California: Four Seasons Foundation, 1973.

Good Accomplishment. Susiddhikara mahātantra sādhanopāyika pa-ṭala. legs par grub par byed pa'i rgyud chen po las sgrub pa'i thabs rim par phye ba. T431.

Good Eon Sutra. Ārya bhadrakalpika nāma mahāyāna sūtra. 'phags pa bskal pa bzang po zhes bya ba theg pa chen po'i mdo. T762.

Good Practice. Ārya bhadracaryā praṇidhāna rāja. 'phags pa bzang po spyod pa'i smon lam gyi rgyal po. T716. Translated by Jes P. Asmussen: *The Khotanese Bhadracaryadeśana*. Copenhagen: Histo-risk-Filosofiske Meddelesser Det Kongelige Danske Videnskabernes Selskab, bind 39, no. 2., 1961.

Heap of Jewels Sutra. Ārya mahāratnakūṭa dharmaparyāya śatasāhasrika grantha. 'phags pa dkon mchog brstegs pa chen po'i chos kyi rnam grangs le'u stong phrag brgyad pa. T760. Partially translated in: *A Treasury of Mahāyāna Sūtras*. Garma C. C. Chang, General Editor. University Park, Pennsylvania: Pennsylvania State University Press, 1983.

Hevajra Tantra. Hevajratantrarāja. khye'i rdo rje zhes bya ba rgyud kyi rgyal po. Toh. 417. Translated by David Snellgrove: *The Hevajra Tantra*. London: Oxford University Press, 1959.

King of Concentrations Sutra. Ārya sarvadharma svabhāva samatāvipañ-cita samādhirāja nāma mahāyāna sūtra. 'phags pa chos kyi thams cad kyi rang bzhin mnyam pa nyid rnam pa spros pa ting nge 'dzin gyi rgyal pa zhes bya ba theg pa chen po'i mdo. T795.

Lion's Roar of Queen Śrīmālā Sutra. Ārya śrīmālā devī siṃhanāda nāma mahāyāna sūtra. 'phags pa lha mo dpal phreng gi seng ge'i sgra zhes bya ba theg pa chen po'i mdo. T760 (48). A chapter of Heap of Jewels Sutra, translated by Alex and Hideko Wayman: *The Lion's Roar of Queen Śrīmālā*. New York and London: Columbia University Press, 1974.

Maitreya's Supplication. Ārya maitreya praṇidhāna. 'phags pa byams pa'i smon lam. T717. A chapter of Heap of Jewels Sutra.

Mother of Conquerors. *See* One Hundred Thousand Verse Transcendent Wisdom Sutra.

One Hundred Thousand Verse Transcendent Wisdom Sutra. Śatasāhasrikā prajñāpāramitā sūtra. shes rab kyi pha rol tu phyin pa stong phrag brgyad pa. T730. The more condensed 25,000 verse version was translated by Edward Conze: *The Large Sutra on Perfect Wisdom*. Berkeley: University of California Press, 1975.

Precious Qualities. New Delhi: International Academy of Indian Culture, 1962.

Proof of Others' Mental Continua. Saṁtānāntara siddhi nāma prakaraṇa. rgyud gzhan grub pa zhes bya ba'i rab tu byed pa. By Dharmakirti. T5716. Translated by Th. Stcherbatsky in: *Papers of Th. Stcherbatsky*. Calcutta: Indian Studies Past and Present, 1969, pp. 81-121.

Purification of the Environment Sutra. Gocana parisuddhi sūtra. spyod yul yongs su dag pa'i mdo. A chapter of the Wreath Sutra.

Royal Sutra of the Inconceivable Secret. Ārya acintya rāja nāma mahāyāna sūtra. 'phags pa bsam gyis mi khyab pa'i rgyal po'i mdo zhes bya ba theg pa chen po'i mdo. T934.

Space Womb Sutra. Ārya ākāśagarbha nāma mahāyāna sūtra. 'phags pa nam mkha'i snying po zhes bya ba theg pa chen po'i mdo. T926.

Sutra Demonstrating the Nonorigination of All Things. Ārya sarvadharmāpravṛtti nirdeśa nāma mahāyāna sūtra. 'phags pa chos tham cad 'byung ba med par bstan pa zhes bya ba theg pa chen po'i mdo. T847.

Sutra Epitomizing All Dharma. Ārya dharma saṁgīti nāma mahāyāna sūtra. 'phags pa chos yang dag par sdud pa zhes bya ba then pa chen po'i mdo. T904.

Sutra on the Great Secret Method. Ārya sarvabuddha mahārahasyopāya kauśalya jñānottara bodhisattva paripṛcchā parivarta nāma mahāyāna sūtra. 'phags pa sang rgyas tham cad kyi gsang chen thabs la mkhas pa byang chub sems dpa' ye shes dam pas zhus pa'i le'u zhes bya ba theg pa chen po'i mdo. T760 (38).

Sutra on the Ten Stages. Daśabhūmika sūtra. sa cu'i mdo. Chapter 31 of Wreath Sutra. T761.

Sutra Requested by Anavatapta. Ārya anavatapta nāgarāja paripṛcchā nāma mahāyāna sūtra. 'phags pa klu'i rgyal po ma dros pas zhus pa zhes bya ba theg pa chen po'i mdo. T823.

Sutra Requested by Kāśyapa. Kāśyapa paripṛcchā sūtra. 'phags pa 'od srung gi le'u zhes bya ba theg pa chen po'i mdo. T760 (43), T765.

Sutra Requested by Rishi Vyasa. Ārya ṛṣivyāsa paripṛcchā nāma mahā-yāna sūtra. 'phags pa drang srong rgyas pas zhus pa zhes bya ba theg pa chen po'i mdo. T760 (49).

Sutra Requested by Sagaramati. Ārya sāgaramati paripṛcchā nāma mahāyāna sūtra. 'phags pa blo gros rgya mtshos zhus pa zhes bya ba theg pa chen po'i mdo. T819.

Sutra Requested by Suvikrāntavikrami. Ārya suvikrāntavikrami pari-pṛcchā prajñāpāramitā nirdeśa. rab gyi rtsal gyis rnam par gnon pas zhus pa shes rab kyo pha rol tu phyin pa bsdan pa. T736. Translated by Edward Conze in: *The Short Prajnaparamita Texts*. London: Luzac & Company Ltd., 1973.

Sutra Requested by Upali. Ārya vinayaviniścaya upāli paripṛcchā nāma mahāyāna sūtra. 'phags pa 'dul ba rnam par gtan la dbab pa nye bar 'khor gyis zhus pa zhes bya ba theg pa chen po'i mdo. T760 (24).

Tantra for Eliminating Lower Births. Sarvadurgati pariśodhana tejorā-jayasya tathāgatasya arhato samyaksambuddhasya kalpa. de bzhin gshegs pa dgra bcom pa yang dag par rdzogs pa'i sangs rgyas ngan song tham cad yongs su sbyong ba gzi brjid kyi rgyal po'i rtog pa zhes bya ba. T116.

Tantra Requested by Subahu. Ārya subāhu paripṛcchā nāma tantra. 'phags pa dpung bzang gis zhus pa zhes bya ba'i rgyud. T428.

Untangling the Knot Sutra. Ārya saṁdhinirmocana nāma mahāyāna sūtra. 'phags pa dgongs pa nges par 'grol pa zhes bya ba theg pa chen po'i mdo. T774. Translated into French by Etienne Lamotte: *Samdhinirmocana Sutra: L'explication des Mystères*. Louvain: Bureaux du Recueil, 1935.

Vairocana's Enlightenment. Mahāvairocanābhisaṁbodhi vikurvitā adhiṣṭhāna vaipulya sūtra indrarāja nāma dharmaparyāya. rnam par snang mdzad chen po mngon par rdzogs par byang cheb par rnam par sprul ba byin gyis rlob pa shin tu rgyas pa mdo sde'i dbang po rgyal po zhes bya ba'i chos kyi rnam grangs. T126. Chapter 1 translated into French by Ryujun Tajima in: *Étude sur le Mahavairocanasutra (Dainichikyo)*. Paris: Adrien Maisonneuve, 1936.

Vajra Tip Tantra. Vajra śekhara mahāguhya yogatantra. gsang ba rnal 'byor chen po'i rgyud rdo rje rtse mo. T113.

Wheel of Time Tantra. Parama adhibuddhoddhṛita śrīkālacakra nāma tantrarāja. mchog gi dang po'i sang rgyas las phyung ba rgyud kyi rgyal po dpal dus kyi 'khor lo zhes bya ba. T4.

Wreath Sutra. Buddha avataṁsaka nāma mahāvaipulya sūtra. sangs rgyas phal po che zhes bya ba shin tu rgyas pa chen po'i mdo. A collection of many sutras. Translated by Thomas Cleary: *The Flower Ornament Scripture*. 3 vols. Boulder, Boston, and London: Shambhala, 1984-87.

2. Texts by Indian and Tibetan Masters (Śāstra)

Accomplishment of Gnosis. Jñāna siddhi nāma sādhana. ye shes grub pa zhes bya ba'i sgrubs thabs. By Indrabhuti. T3063.

Analysis of the Middle and the Extremes. Madhyānta vighaṅga. dbus dang mtha' rnam par 'byed pa. By Maitreyanatha. T5522. Translated by Th. Stcherbatsky: *Madhyāntavibhaṅga: Discourse on Discrimination between the Middle and the Extreme*. Moscow-Leningrad: Bibliotheca Buddhica, no. 30, 1938.

Birth Stories. Jātakamālā. skyes pa'i rabs kyi rgyud. By Āryasūra. T5650. Translated by J. S. Speyer: *The Jātakamālā: or Garland of Birth Stories of Āryaśūra*. Delhi: Motilal Banarsidass, 1971.

The Bodhisattva's Stages. Bodhisattvabhūmi. byang chub sems pa'i sa. By Asanga.

Commentary on Crown of Great Vehicle Sutras. Sūtrālaṁkāravyākhyā. mdo sde'i rgyan gyi bshad pa. By Vasubandhu. Toh.4026

Commentary on the Sixty Verses of Reasoning. Yuktiṣaṣṭikā vṛtti. rigs pa drug bcu pa'i 'grel ba. By Candrakīrti. T5265.

Compendium of Ascertainment. Yogacaryā bhūmi nirṇaya saṁgraha. rnal 'byor spyod pa'i sa rnam par gtan la dbab pa bsdu ba. By Asaṅga. T5539.

Crown of Great Vehicle Sutras. Mahāyāna sūtrālaṁkāra. theg pa chen po mdo sde rgyan. By Maitreya. Translated into French by Sylvan Levi: *Mahayanasutralamkara: Exposé de la doctrine du Grand Véhicule selon le systeme Yogacara*. 2 vols. Paris: Champion, 1907-11.

Crown of Realizations. Abhisamayālaṁkāra nāma prajñāpāramitopadeśa śāstra kārikā. shes rab kyi pha rol tu phyin pa'i nam ngag gi bstan bcos mngon par rtogs pa'i rgyan zhes bya ba'i tshig le'ur byas pa. By Maitreya. T5184. Translated by Edward Conze: *Abhisamayālaṁ* kāra: *Introduction and Translation from the Original Text*. Roma: Instituto Italiano per il Medio ed Estremo Oriente, 1954.

Devotee's Eightfold Vow. Upasaka saṁvarāṣṭaka. dge bsnyen gyi sdom pa brgyad pa. By Śūnyaśrī. T5642.

Digest of the Great Vehicle. Mahāyāna saṁgraha. theg pa chen pa bsdus pa. By Asaṅga. T5549. Translated by Etienne Lamotte: *La Somme du Grand Véhicule d'Asanga*. Louvain: Bureaux du Museon, 1938.

Discipline Sutra. Vinayasūtra. 'dul ba'i mdo. By Guṇaprabha. T5619.

Encyclopedia of Illuminating Science. Abhidharma samuccaya. chos mngon pa kun las btus pa. By Asaṅga. T5550.

Entering the Bodhisattva's Practice. Bodhisattvacaryāvatāra. byang chub sems dpa'i spyod pa la 'jug pa. By Śāntideva. T5272. Translated by Steven Batchelor: *A Guide to the Bodhisattva's Way of Life*. Dharamsala: Library of Tibetan Works and Archives, 1979.

Entering the Middle Way. Madhyamakāvatāra kārikā. bdu ma la 'jug pa'i tshig le'ur byas pa. By Candrakīrti. T5261. [Autocommentary: Madhyamakāvatāra bhāṣya, dbu ma la 'jug pa'i bshad pa. T5263.]

Epitome of Precepts. Śikṣā samuccaya. bslab pa kun las btus pa. By Śāntideva. T5336. Translated by Cecil Bandall and W. H. D. Rouse: *Sikshāsamuccaya: A Compendium of Buddhist Doctrine*. Delhi: Motilal Banarsidass, 1971.

Epitome of Purification of the Environment. Bodhisattva gocara pariśuddhi sūtrārtha saṁgraha. byang chub sems dpa'i spyod yul yongs su dags pa'i mdo don mdor bsdus pa. By Rāhulabhadra [Attributed to Jñānagarbha by Sakya Pandita]. T5360. [The Tibetan version found in the canon does not contain the excerpt quoted. A text of the same title by Jñānagarbha may exist but not be included in the canon.]

Essential Wisdom. Mūlamadhyamaka kārikā. dbu ma rtsa ba'i tshig le'ur shes rab ces bya ba. By Nāgārjuna. T5224. Translated by Kenneth K. Inada: *Nāgārjuna: A Translation of his Mūlamadhyamakakārikā with an Introductory Essay*. Tokyo: The Hokuseido Press, 1970.

Exposition of Valid Cognition. Pramāṇavārttika kārikā. tshad ma rnam par 'grel ba tshig le'ur byas pa. By Dharmakīrti. T5709. Chapter 1 translated by S. Mokerjee and Hojun Nagasaki: *The Pramāṇavārttikam of Dharmakīrti*. Nalanda: Nava Nalanda Mahavira, 1964.

Five Maitreya Books. The works given by Maitreya to Asaṅga while he was meditating. They are: Crown of Realizations, Crown of Great

Vehicle Sutras, Analysis of the Mean and the Extreme, Analysis of the Phenomenal and the Real, and Peerless Principle of the Great Vehicle. See separate entries.

Five Stages. Pañcakrama. Rim pa lnga pa. By Nāgārjuna. T2667.

Four Hundred Verses. Catuḥśataka śāstra kārikā. bstan bcos bzhi brgya pa zhes bya ba'i tshig le'ur byas ba. By Āryadeva. T5246. Partially translated into English by V. Battacharya in: *Proceedings of the All-India Oriental Conference*, vol. 4, 1928, pp. 831-81.

Friendly Letter to the King. Suhṛllekha. bshes pa'i spring yig. By Nāgārjuna. T5409, T5682. Translated by H. V. Guenther and Leslie Kawamura in: *Golden Zephyr*. Emeryville, California: Dharma Publishing, 1975.

Great Stages of the Mantric Path. By Tsongkapa. Partially translated by Jeffrey Hopkins in: *Tantra in Tibet*. London: George Allen & Unwin, 1977.

Great Stages of the Path. By Tsongkapa.

In Praise of Special Superiority. Viśeṣa stava. khyad par du 'phags pa'i bstod pa. By Udbhatasiddhasvamin. T2001.

Jātaka Stories. *See* Birth Stories.

Jewel Ornament of Liberation. By Gampopa. Translated by H. V. Guenther. Berkeley: Shambala Publications, 1971.

Lamp of the Path to Enlightenment. Bodhipathapradīpa. byan chub lam gyi sgron ma. By Atisa. Toh.3947, 4465.

Maxims of King Canakya. Cāṇakya nīti śāstra. tsa na ka'i lugs kyi bstan bcos. By Cāṇakya. T5826.

Meditation on the Intent for Enlightenment. Bodhicittotpādavidhi. byang chub tu sems bskyed pa'i cho ga. By Nāgārjuna. Toh.3966, 4492.

Peerless Principle [of the Great Vehicle]. Mahāyānottaratantra śāstra. theg pa chen po rgyud bla ma'i bstan bcos. By Maitreya. T5525. Translated by Jikido Takasaki: *A Study of the Ratnagotravibhaga (Uttaratantra)*. Roma: Instituto Italiano per il Medio ed Estremo Oriente, 1966; and by Katia Holmes and Ken Tsultrim Gyamtso: *The Changeless Nature*. Dumfriesshire, Scotland: Karma Drubgyud Darjay Ling, n.d. [1983].

Precious Garland. Rāja parikathā ratnamālā. rgyal po la gtam bya ba rin po che'i phreng ba. By Nāgārjuna. T5658. Translated by Jeffrey

Hopkins and Lati Rinpoche in: *The Precious Garland and the Song of the Four Mindfulnesses*. New York: Harper & Row, 1975.

Sixty Verses of Reasoning. Yuktiṣaṣṭikā kārikā. lta ba ngan pa sel ba zhes bya ba. By Advayavajra. T3073.

Stages of a Bodhisattva's Practice. Bodhisattvabhūmi. byang chub sems dpa'i sa. By Āsaṅga. Toh.4037.

Treasury of Illuminating Science. Abhidharmakośa kārikā. chos mngon pa mdzod kyi tshig le'ur byas pa. By Vasubandhu. T5590. [Autocommentary: Abhidharmakośa bhāṣya, chos mngon pa mdzod kyi bshad pa, T5591.] Translated into French by Louis Vallee Poussin: *L'Abhidharmakośa de Vasubandhu*. 6 vols. Paris: Paul Guenther, 1923-31.

Twenty Verses. Mahāyānaviṃśakā. theg pa chen po nyi shu pa. By Nāgārjuna. T5233. Translated by V. Bhattacharya in: *Visvabharati Quarterly*, vol. 8. 1930-31, pp. 107-150; and by G. Tucci in *Minor Buddhist Texts*, Roma: Instituto Italiano per il Medio ed Estremo Oriente, 1956.

Twenty Vows. Bodhisattva saṃvara vimśaka. byang chub sems dpa'i sdom pa nyi shu pa. By Candragomin. T5582.

Wish Granting Vine Teaching the Bodhisattva's Realizations. Bodhisattvāvadāna kalpalatā. byang chub sems pa'i rtogs pa brjod pa'i dpag bsam gyi 'khri shing. By Kṣemendra. T5655.

3. *Works of Sakya Authors*

Precious Treasury of Elegant Sayings. legs par bshad pa rin po che'i gter. By Sakya Pandita. *Complete Works*. vol. 5, *tha* 100-122a. Translated by J. E. Bosson: *A Treasury of Aphoristic Jewels*. Bloomington: Indiana University, Indiana University Publications, Uralic and Altaic Series, vol. 92, 1969; and revised in *Elegant Sayings*. Emeryville, California: Dharma Publishing, 1977.

Ritual for Production of the Intent for Enlightenment of the Middle Way School and Its Commentary. dbu ma lugs kyi sems bskyed kyi cho ga, 'grel ba. By Sakya Pandita. *Complete Works*, vol. 5, 21-22, 221-239, 264-273.

Treasury of Logic. tshad ma rigs pa'i gter. By Sakya Pandita. *Complete Works*. vol. 5, *da* 1-25a.

Glossary

Absorption, absorption levels (*dhyāna*) The distinct, metastable states of mental operation attained through tranquilization of mental functioning by one-pointed concentration. Attainment of the eight successively more quiescent absorption levels—the first four comprising the form realm and the second four the formless realm—involves the suppression of thought and disturbing mental functions. Their duration depends on the force of the process of suppression. They are states common to all yoga and are entirely samsaric in nature.

Accomplishments (*siddhi*) Supernormal abilities or powers developed in the course of advanced practice.

Action (*karma*) Exactly that; any intentional or unintentional action performed through the "three doors": body, speech, and mind. There are three types: virtuous, yielding positive results; evil, yielding negative results; and fixed, which refers to action in a state of absorption that yields results that are "fixed" or limited to the absorption levels.

Aggregates (*phung po*) The body and mind are made up of five aggregates: form, feeling, perceptions, mental functions, and consciousness.

Akaniṣṭha heaven Abode of a bodhisattva just prior to birth in the world where he or she is to achieve final buddhahood.

Analytic insight (*vipasyana*) The process of detailed examination of the meditation object as to its actual mode of existence. It involves thought and is aimed at penetrating the conceptual process; it results in tolerance to the direct perception of voidness.

Appearance, apparent world (*snang ba*) Reality as it appears to a common individual whose conditioned, distorted perception experiences reality in the form of discrete, independent identities. Synonym: illusory world, superficial reality.

Arhat (*dgra bcom pa*) In the lesser vehicle system, one who has obtained the highest attainment, the culmination of the four stages of perfection: stream winner, once-returner, nonreturner, arhatship (the conquest of inner defilements). In the great vehicle system disciples and solitary buddhas attain arhatship when they reach the fifth of the five paths, the path of no more learning (*mi slob lam*).

Basic process (*ālayavijñāna*) The eighth consciousness, according to the Mind Only school developed by Asaṅga in the fifth century. It is the basic substratum of the individual's consciousness that carries the imprintings of "seeds" of past and future experience.

Bodhisattva Literally, "enlightenment warrior"; dedicated to spiritual advancement and liberation to help others in their own development. To become a bodhisattva a person must generate the intent for enlightenment, or great compassion, and have some experience of the inherent voidness of self and world.

Cognitive patterning *see* Patterning.

Compulsive (*upadāna*) Automatic, habitual—in reference to the patterning of mental functioning—involving perceptions, thought, and emotional reactions, according to the conditionings of past experience.

Concentration (*samādhi*) The technique of controlling the mechanisms of attention through the focusing of attention on a single object. It is a development of the inherent capacity to "pay attention" and is a basic prerequisite for all advanced practices, such as analytic or introspective techniques.

Dependent origination (*pratītya-samutpāda*) The twelve linked causal factors involved in the cycle of samsaric existence. In basic buddhism, it refers to the succession and circumstances of rebirths, and in later thought is applied also to the production of each cognition of any phenomenal thing.

Disciple (*śrāvaka*) The disciples of Buddha Śākyamuni and the followers of their schools. There were eighteen such schools in India whose teachings comprise the lesser vehicle. In the specific sense it refers to persons who have attained arhatship.

Eight pressured situations (*mi khom brgyad*) Birth as a hell being, as an animal, as a hungry ghost (*preta*), as a long-lived god, birth among uncivilized people, with defective faculties, strong wrong views, and birth into a world where a buddha has not yet appeared.

Empowerment (*abhiṣeka*) Conferral of the inspiration and instructions for a practice; in particular, the four major tantric empowerments—called the *vase* or *pot*, the *secret*, *wisdom*, and *word*—which are directed toward development of body, speech, mind, and insight into ultimate reality, respectively.

Enlightenment (*bodhi*) The state of buddhahood constituted by perfection of the two stores and removal of the two obscurations. It is the only level of attainment beyond the range of samsara.

Fabrication, mental (*prapañca*) The internal stream of conceptualization directed by imprinted preconceptions. The term includes both the internal flow of thought constructs and the self and environment they "create."

Form body (*rūpakāya*) Term for the enjoyment and emanation bodies together. (*See* Three Bodies.)

Four classes of tantra (*rgyud bzhi*) The canon of the mantrayāna. They are: *kriyātantra* (*bya ba'i rgyud*), *caryātantra* (*spyad pa'i rgyud*), *yogatantra* (*rnal 'byor ba'i rgyud*), and *annuttarayogatantra* (*rnal 'byor la na med pa'i rgyud*). The fourth is the highest.

Four devils (*māra*) Samsaric enemies to liberation; they are: one's psychophysical constituents, afflictive mental states, death, and external obstructions.

Four infinitudes (*apramāna*) Basic emotions that can be developed into catalysts for generating the mind aimed at enlightenment (*bodhicitta*). They are: love, compassion, joy, and mental equanimity.

Four noble truths They are: that suffering is inherent in existence; that there is a cause of this suffering; that this suffering can be stopped, that the way to stop this suffering is the truth of the superior path. This is the teaching of the first wheel of Dharma.

Four phases conducive to penetration The phases or processes of warmth, peak, tolerance, and supreme mundane state which constitute the application path.

Great vehicle (*mahāyāna*) *see* Vehicle.

Identity (*svabhāva*) The "intrinsic identifiability" of anything. The ordinary mind compartmentalizes its experience into objects appearing to be independent entities. The inherent lack of identity in persons and things constitutes voidness, their true mode of existence.

Illuminating Science (*abhidharma*) The third basket of the buddhist canon (*tripiṭaka*). The systematized philosophical and psychological analysis of existence that is the basis for the buddhist systems of tenets and mind training.

Imprint (*vāsanā*) The mental traces of past experience and action which give rise to the present samsaric situation.

Intent for enlightenment (*bodhicitta*) The intent to attain one's own enlightenment to help liberate others. It is not the state of enlightenment itself, but the selfless drive to attain it for the sake of others. In the great vehicle it is the necessary complement to the penetrating insight into voidness and in the tantric vehicle the prerequisite to real practice.

Karma *see* Action.

Mahāmudrā "Great Gesture" or "Great Seal." An advanced practice closely aligned with the peerless (*anuttara*) yoga tantras; aimed at direct revelation of the natural reality of the apparent world.

Method (*upaya*) The active expression of the intent for enlightenment (*bodhicitta*). It is the complement of transcendent wisdom that balances its intense revelations and that the bodhisattva uses to relate to beings, skillfully turning each situation into an opportunity for advancement for all.

Mundane (*laukika*) Perceptions, thoughts, emotions, and states of mind that occur under the influence of the conditioning or imprinting of past experience; the apparent world.

Natural state (*gnas lug*) The natural mode of existence of all things; the mental state wherein experience is not distorted by preconceived perceptions of identities.

Nirvana (*nirvana*) The cessation of one's own misery through eradication of afflictional mental states. In the great vehicle *nirvana* is used in distinction to *enlightenment*, which involves not only the eradication of misery but also the attainment of unique abilities and insights into reality.

Obscuration (*āvaraṇa*) A term that includes all conditionings under two categories of emotional or afflictive obscuration and cognitive obscuration. The afflictional obscuration (*kleśa-avāraṇa*) consists of negative mental states that obscure nirvana's freedom from misery. The objective obscuration (*jñeya-avāraṇa*) consists of fundamental misperceptions of the world which obscure perfect enlightenment.

Patterning (*vikālpa*) The structuring of cognition caused by the traces of past experience; this patterning gives rise to the apparent world of self and environment and all our emotional reactions to such appearances.

Personal diety (*yi dam*) Figures of the tantric pantheon who embody particular mental states and the practices leading to transformation of the practitioner's mind into the "mind of the diety." Usually a practitioner has a relationship with a single diety, based on his personal nature and aims, although others may also be involved in practice over time. Through correct empowerment, instructions, and visualization meditation, a practitioner eventually experiences the diety and his mental reality.

Postrealization state The state immediately following any direct, transcendent experience of voidness, called "actual realization state." During the actual realization state the perception of the apparent world yields to the perception of its voidness, whereas in the postattainment state the preconceived perception of the apparent world returns subtly altered by the preceding experience.

Seven acts of worship (*pūjā*) Salutation, offerings, confession, rejoicing in the accomplishments of others, asking the buddhas to remain and teach, requesting blessings, and dedication of the merit of the *pūjā* to all beings.

Sign (*lakṣaṇā*) Distinguishing characteristic of an object that calls up a particular conceptualization.

Solitary buddha (*pratyekabuddha*) A person of the lesser vehicle who has attained nirvana for his own benefit without the aid of a buddha's teaching.

Superficial reality (*saṃvṛtisatya*) Also called relative truth or relative reality. The world as it appears when perception is conditioned by verbal conventions. The term "reality" emphasizes the fact that, owing to its relative self-consistency, it does appear to be a valid reality to ordinary beings.

Superior (*ārya*) A person who has experienced voidness and has thus attained the "path of insight."

Tantra (*rgyud*) Scriptures of Śākyamuni and other buddhas relating to tantric, or esoteric, practice.

Tathagata (*tathāgata*) Epithet of a buddha; literally, "one who has gone there."

Ten vices (*akuśala*) The ten main vices are: killing, stealing, sexual misconduct, lying, slander, abusive speech, senseless speech, coveting, ill-will, and wrong views. The ten main virtues are abstaining from these vices.

Three bodies (*trikāya*) The three modes of existence and communication for an enlightened being. Dharma body, or reality body, is the embodiment of voidness and its realization; the enjoyment body is the means of communication with advanced meditators; and the emanation body appears like a physical body in the world, but its form and activities are consciously directed and consist of the training of undeveloped beings. A fourth body, the essential body, represents the unity of the above three.

Three concepts The threefold concept of agent, action, and recipient of action.

Three disciplines The general categories of moral behavior, concentration, and wisdom, which include all buddhist practices.

Three Jewels (*triratna*) The refuge sources of buddhism: the Buddha, representing enlightenment, the Dharma, his teachings, and the Sangha, the Community of practictioners.

Three vehicles (*yāna*) The term "vehicle" connotes a means of traveling to enlightenment, that is, a major system of teaching and practice. The lesser vehicle is the oldest, relying on the scriptures set down in Pali. The great vehicle includes the teachings of the lesser vehicle, but in a new context and expanded scope. The tantric vehicle (vajra vehicle, mantra vehicle) combines the outlook of the great vehicle with a radically different, high-powered system of practice.

Three wisdoms The wisdoms derived from learning, reflecting on what was learned, and meditating with the principles thus considered, comprise all knowledge and realization in the course of development. The first two are termed "mundane" because they are not transcendent, consisting of facts learned from reliable sources and those derived from rational consideration of those facts. When such correctly considered facts are applied in meditation, the resultant transcendent realization experiences are termed "wisdom derived from meditation."

Trace *see* Imprint.

Tranquilization (*śamatha*) The systematic quieting of mental activity through practice of one-pointed concentration. It is the means of attaining the eight absorption levels and the prerequisite for proper practice of analytic insight.

Transcendences Sometimes known as "perfections." The complex of practices that are the basis of mahāyāna practice. For this reason the *mahāyāna* is also referred to as the *pāramitāyāna*—"vehicle of the transcendences." They form an integrated system of behavioral and mental techniques for initiating, developing, and focusing energy and activity from the beginning of practice until buddhahood. They are listed as six or ten.

Transcendent (*lokattara*) Mental events or experiences beyond the world of conditioned appearances (in other words, the experience of voidness).

Two accumulations *see* Two stores.

Two phases (*krama*) The two stages of tantric practice. The first, the production phase (*utpattikrama*), involves the visualized production of the tantric deities and their domains. The second, the completion phase (*utpannakrama*), is the completion of this process by penetrating the voidness of all appearances. It utilizes inner psychic control of winds, channels, and drops.

Two realities *see* Two truths.

Two stages *see* Two phases.

Two stores (*sambhāra*) The two accumulations of personal power: the store of merit based on ethical behavior and ritual, and the store of gnosis based on knowledge and wisdom. When completed, the two stores provide the necessary elements utilized in achieving direct experience of voidness.

Two truths All objects of cognition have two modes of existence, called truths: the truth of appearance, relative truth (*saṃvṛtisatya*), is the aspect of existence according to worldly convention and expression, and absolute truth (*paramāthasatya*) is the voidness of all phenomena, the reality of existence.

Valid cognition (*pramāṇa*) Cognition that is nonerroneous in a relative sense. It consists of two types: direct perception and inference or conceptual cognition. Direct perceptions may be those of the sensory processes, the central process, apperceptive, and yogic, which occurs only in the transcendent cognition of a superior.

Voidness (*śūnyata*) The actual nature of all things; the lack of any independent ego of persons and identity of things.

Wisdom (*prajñā*) Generally, any correct knowledge. Specifically, transcendent wisdom, the direct perception of the void nature of persons and things. During such experience the perception of the apparent world is temporarily suppressed.

Index

Numbers appearing in the index in boldface refer to glossary terms.